BANNER BRIGHT

Dedicated to my father, 1903-1984,
sixty-one years a member of
the Amalgamated Society of Woodworkers
and the Union of Construction, Allied Trades and Technicians.

Look, my comrades, see the union
Banners waving high;
Reinforcements now appearing,
Victory is nigh.

Hold the fort, for we are coming,
Union men, be strong.
Side by side we battle onward,
Victory will come.*

* Originally a song of the American Knights of Labour in the
1880s, 'Storm the fort, ye Knights of Labour', given its present
form by the Transport Workers of Britain and sung again during
the great miners' strike of 1972.

BANNER BRIGHT

AN ILLUSTRATED HISTORY OF TRADE UNION BANNERS

JOHN GORMAN

INTRODUCTION BY GWYN A. WILLIAMS
FOREWORD BY NORMAN WILLIS

SCORPION PUBLISHING LTD

BANNER BRIGHT
NEW EDITION 1986

© TEXT · JOHN GORMAN 1973 AND 1986
© PHOTOGRAPHS · JOHN GORMAN UNLESS OTHERWISE
STATED IN THE ACKNOWLEDGEMENTS
© INTRODUCTION · GWYN A. WILLIAMS 1973 AND 1986
FIRST PUBLISHED IN 1973 BY ALLEN LANE
THIS EDITION IS COMPLETELY REVISED, REPRINTED,
RESET AND ENLARGED AND IS PUBLISHED BY
SCORPION PUBLISHING LTD
VICTORIA HOUSE · VICTORIA ROAD
BUCKHURST HILL · ESSEX · ENGLAND

ISBN 0 905906 49 7 CASED
ISBN 0 905906 48 9 PAPER

A SCORPION PICA PRODUCTION

EDITOR · LEONARD HARROW
HOUSE EDITOR · JOHN ORLEY
ART EDITORS · JOHN GORMAN AND COLIN LARKIN
DESIGN AND ART DIRECTION · COLIN LARKIN
TYPESETTING · CHRISTINE CROSSMAN AND JOHN ORLEY
STUDIO ASSISTANT · SUSAN PIPE
SET IN LINOTYPE NEW BASKERVILLE
PAPER · ROYAL SWORD MATT ART 135GSM
PRINTING AND BINDING · HAZELL WATSON AND VINEY LTD · ENGLAND

CONTENTS

ACKNOWLEDGEMENTS

I owe a special debt of gratitude to the hundreds of trade unionists who met me with kindness and brotherly help wherever I travelled in my search to find and record the banners of this great movement. My deepest thanks are also due to George Groves, Sid Brown, Ted Brake, Ken Sprague and Imogen Forster for their encouragement and practical help with this work.

Finally, a personal and special thanks to my wife Pamela for all the banners she has held and unfurled and for her infinite patience in living with the clutter and talk of banners for four years.

In this revised edition, I would like to extend my belated thanks to Ann Proctor for typing the original manuscript. I am grateful too for the help given by Eve Denney in typing my amended text and to Lisa Collins for typing my correspondence. It is a matter of regret that I did not list by name all those who helped with the first edition, for they made an invaluable contribution to labour history. It is with appreciation I acknowledge the following individuals and organisations that have willingly cooperated in making this new version of *Banner Bright* possible: Phil Barley, Beamish, North of England Open Air Museum, Ray Bishop, Blaise Castle House Museum, Bristol, Ted Brake, Sid Brown, Margaret Burlton, Campbell Design, Chippenham Designs, Mrs D. Clark, Corby Community Arts Association, County Reference Library, Bristol, Dave Douglas, Bill Dowding, Graham Downie, Peter Duffy, Museum and Art Gallery, Dundee, Andy Durr, Chris Ecclestone, R.L. Hookes, Huntly House Museum, Edinburgh, Allan Hutchison, Hywell Francis, Phil James, Ray James, E. Killick, J. Kinahan, Kirkcaldy Museums and Art Gallery, P.R. Lowman, C.A. Lyons, Ian MacDougall, Brian Massie, Ron McKillop, H. Mindel, Jack Moss, W.A. Moyes, National Museum of Labour History, Jock Nimmo, *Northern Echo*, Oxford County Library, The People's Palace, Glasgow, Mick Richmond, Jane Roberts, Roxburgh District Council, The Royal West of England Academy, Regan Scott, W. Scott, Colin Sheehan, Barney Shuster, John Smethurst, Alec Smith, J.R. Smith, Ken Street, Tricia Sumner, Colin Talbot, Gareth Thomas, Town Docks Museum, Hull, TUC Library, Andrew Turner, Janet Vitmayer, Sonya Walters, Daphne Waterton, Margaret Wheeler, Ulster Museum, Belfast, Wilton Lodge Museum, Hawick, Dennis Whysall, Danny Williamson.

Finally, I would like to record my thanks to Allen Lane, who, declining to reprint the book, generously made the photographic film, including the colour separations, available to Scorpion Publishing.

John Gorman
May 1986

FOREWORD

As General Secretary of the TUC, I am delighted to be writing the foreword to *Banner Bright*. Trade union banners are the most vivid and colourful part of our heritage; no demonstration, no march, no rally would be complete without them. They tell our story in a way that celebrates the unity of the trade union movement. The struggles and campaigns have been hard fought, and often bitter; but the colours and brilliance of the banners proclaim the pride working people have in their unions, and the consciousness that they have become, through those unions, a real force in the land.

One of the great strengths of the British trade union movement has always been its diversity. I believe this has given us a strength and a moral authority lacking in those movements which are split along political or ideological lines. This diversity is reflected in many of the banners. A movement which can march behind so many different banners but still be a united and cohesive force has, to quote one banner, 'many minds, but one heart' and will always be a force to be reckoned with.

It is not only working poeple's pride in their unions which is depicted on the banners; it is their pride in the work itself. The book is replete with images of factories, coalmines, steamtrains, ships and the tools and instruments of many trades. Historically, the image of Britain as 'the workshop of the world' has tended to focus exclusively on the industrialists and the entrepreneurs, and they played their part. But it was in the mines and the mills and the factories where the work was done that the wealth was created – and by people who saw all too little of the fruits of that wealth. The images of this work, so proudly woven on the banners, have a special poignancy today, when so many of the industries have been allowed to collapse, and the skills and talents of so many of our people are being wasted on the dole.

A point which will occur to anyone reading the book is the extent to which so many of the images and slogans depicted on the banners concern battles which many of us thought were long won, but which we are now having to re-fight to prevent so many of our people once again falling victim to the anarchy of the free market; even the very right to belong to a trade union is under attack. As we unfurl those banners again, we remind ourselves, as one of them does, that 'eternal vigilance is the price of freedom!'

Banner Bright does great service to the trade union movement. It vividly reminds us of our history and our heritage, and of the struggle and sacrifice that went to make up that history. It reminds us of the principles that inspire the trade union movement, and of the commitment of generations of trade unionists to those principles. It deserves to be widely read – as I am sure it will be.

Norman Willis
May 1986

PREFACE

When *Banner Bright* was first published on May Day, 1973, it seemed that the art and tradition of making and parading trade union banners had declined to such an extent that we had reached the end of this peculiarly British form of working class culture. It was possible to contrast the May Day parades of the late nineteenth century, when trade union banners flying high above the cobbled streets were counted in hundreds, to 1970, when the official Labour Party May Day celebration took place at the Festival Hall, London, without a banner to be seen. However, since then, there has been a steady resurgence of the mass appearance of union iconography on the streets of Britain and a diversification and spread of the art of the banner maker.

Before the abrupt decline in the 1960s, banner making had enjoyed a brief period of regeneration following the end of the Second World War, especially among the miners. The spirit of the imagery was optimism, celebration of Labour's great victory, the materialisation of Walter Crane's vision of the 'The triumph of labour'. The banners hailed nationalisation as 'The dawn of a new era' (Risca lodge), proclaimed it as the rightful appropriation of 'Our heritage' (Harton and Westoe lodge) and listed the rapid achievements of Labour, 'Social Security', Family Allowances, Nationalisation, Five-day Week, Health, 'Peace and Prosperity', and anticipated the final goal of socialism (North Gawber lodge and others). The heroes were Attlee, Bevan, Cripps, Dalton, Bevin and Shinwell (Morrison seems to have been ignored and 'Red Ellen' Wilkinson the victim of male prejudice), their portraits emblazoned on the banners in acclamation of victory. 'We are the masters now', if apocryphal was the mood of the moment. For the veterans of 1921 and 1926, those with bitter memories of years of poverty and unemployment, 'the long, long night' was over, neatly summed up by the inscription on the banner of Dysart lodge 'Anticipation 1888, Desperation 1921-26, Realisation 1943, Nationalisation 1947'.

The future, vividly captured by the visual imagery on scores of banners, was a land of well-fed children, nurtured on free milk and school dinners, tidy brick suburban council houses, a decent life for old people, fair shares for all and a land of new technology easing the burden of labour and increasing leisure. The motto on the banner of Westoe lodge echoed the confidence of fulfilment, 'We are the far-off future of the distant past. We are the noble race for whom they dreamed and died'. 'Pioneers, o pioneers', who could doubt the day had arrived?

Just how the golden dream was allowed to slip from such a firm grasp will long be argued. So far as the history of the banners of our trade union movement is concerned, the defeat of Labour in 1951 virtually halted a tradition built over a period of 150 years. The banners lay neglected in damp basements, beneath the stages of dusty Labour halls, crumpled beneath cardboard fileboxes of ancient minutes in cramped cupboards. The colourful pride of generations left to crumble. Yet as I write, the tradition of banner carrying flourishes, nowhere better witnessed than in the great demonstrations of support for the miners during their heroic struggle in the 1984-5 strike. Resurgence may be said to have begun with the TUC-organised 'Great March' on 21 February 1971 against the Conservative government's Industrial Relations Bill. The parade of banners, many on their first outing for twenty years or more, caught the eyes of a new generation of trade unionists, especially those in the fast-growing public service unions.

With the carefully planned dismantling of the Welfare State by successive Thatcher governments, the bargain offers of the people's industries to private capital, the return of mass unemployment, the most vicious anti-trade union legislation since 1927 and the destruction of British manufacturing industry, there has emerged a proliferation of new banners, with a new militancy. Amid the undoubted defeatism, disillusionment and despondency to be found in wide sections of the labour movement, there has blossomed a fresh, vigorous iconography that challenges the assumptions of Thatcher's popular capitalism. Black and white workers appear together in unity (National Union of Public Employees and National Association of Local Government Officers in particular), women are depicted as manual workers, the influence of the women's movement having swept away the bare-breasted allegorical maidens of yesterday, there is a rejection of racism (Newcastle branch of the Civil and Public Services Association), workers are depicted wearing the familiar black and white badge of CND (AUEW West London District Committee) and the red flag is seen flying over the House of Lords (Transport and General Workers' Union, Parliamentary branch). Popular left slogans, 'The workers, united, will never be defeated', appear in place of familiar mottoes and clenched fists are as commonplace as the clasped handshake.

The pattern of banner imagery, shaped by George Tutill, has finally been changed, but not entirely discarded. Trade unionists still have a deep pride in the products of their labours or the services they provide. If the silicon chip and Concorde (Transport and General Workers' Union, Birmingham Power and Engineering District Committee) have replaced the hammer and coach as symbols of craft pride and identity, the spirit is unaltered. Whatever the work, there is dignity in labour as acknowledged by the portrayal of a dustman on the Newcastle-upon-Tyne banner of NUPE. Nurses and steelworkers, builders and miners, teachers and clerks, all and every type of worker are still painted proudly on the banners of the organised working class. Other traditions also linger, with the portraits of the miners' president, Arthur Scargill, adorning the banners of more than one branch of the NUM. Work, leadership and socialist ideals remain central as the major theme of contemporary trade union banners.

It is the challenging ideas of rank and file branch members linked to a committed and imaginative response by young and independent artists that has brought an exciting freshness to the form of contemporary banner art. If the skilful professionalism of the experienced banner maker is sometimes missing from the end product, this is compensated, at least in the short term, by the immediacy and originality of the new imagery. While the old established firms of banner makers like Turtle and Pearce (the successors to George Tutill) and the famous regalia company of Toye, Kenning and Spencer continue to produce traditional banners of the highest quality, with a corresponding longer life, it is the dedicated individuals and small firms who are pioneering the 'new look' in design, materials and technique. The appliqué methods favoured by Thalia Campbell, Ken Sprague and others, the strip method for easy transportation developed by John Dugger, both represent innovation in the production of union banners. Likewise, the too often stereotyped form of the commercial banner manufacturer is rejected by artists like Conrad Atkinson and Andrew Turner. Of course, there are some trade unionists who prefer the familiar patterns of the past, clinging to the ornate romanticism of the nineteenth century, but they are losing ground to a young generation of

trade unionists with their own ideas of working class expression.

If we have no need to copy the past, we have the duty to preserve it for future generations as a reminder of our heritage, created and shaped in struggle amid poverty and adversity. The *Banner Bright* exhibition of trade union banners held at the Whitechapel Art Gallery, London, and at provincial galleries in 1973 acted as a catalyst in creating an appreciation of the value of these irreplaceable relics. The deliberate destruction and disposal of old banners has for the most part been halted and enthusiasts for trade union history in all parts of Britain continually make new discoveries. Most museums now recognise the social and historic worth of their local banners and many trade unions have awakened to the importance of the relics they hold in trust. However, with the long and rich history of the British labour movement we find ourselves bequeathed with scores, if not hundreds, of vintage banners; the problem is how and where they should be preserved. We must be realistic and accept that we do not have the current resources to effect an adequate conservation policy in the immediate future. Better therefore that we should concentrate on the proper care of the oldest, rarest and historically most important. Progress has been made in the field of preservation and conservation, stimulated by the growing interest in the value of visual labour history, but we are only beginning. The tragedy is that too few organisations have any concept or knowledge as to what is required for the long-term preservation of our historic banners. Too many are openly hung to disintegrate slowly as sunlight, heat, dust, organisms and the chemical action of paint on silk eat away at the very fabric. To some, restoration is paramount and effected by a hideous re-painting of faded banners, without any thought as to what they are supposed to be preserving, unless it be a crude forgery. To the restorationists I commend the writings of William Morris on 'anti-scrape'. Lethaby recounts how Morris, enraged by a thoroughly 'restored' church, rushed to the window and 'shook his fist as the parson passed by'. More than one curator has provoked the same feelings within myself. For the conservationists, perhaps it is time we formed a Society for the Preservation of Ancient Banners!

If the most ancient, rare and important of our banners are to be preserved for hundreds of years it is no good simply hanging them on open display. Apart from intelligent conservation, they need to be stored flat, out of natural light and only exhibited in a strictly controlled environment for limited periods of time. This need not be a deprivation given modern methods of reproduction such as the Scanachrome process, enabling facsimiles of the most valuable banners to be displayed in conjunction with actual banners of lesser importance. Even with the popular banners that proliferated since 1890, great care and thought needs to be given to public display if they are to last for another fifty years or so. They should be protected from harmful ultra-violet light, detrimental to the silk and pigments alike, the fabric restored to ensure adequate support for the weight of the banner, sensibly cleaned and displayed where they are not subjected to constant handling.

It makes sense to keep them where they relate to the community. What useful purpose is to be served by housing Scottish banners in London or vice versa? Museums of labour history, local museums, libraries, civic offices and trade union buildings, all can provide a suitable home for local banners. Here I make a plea that trade unions should not rush to surrender all their old banners to institutions, for they still belong to their members. There is no reason why an old banner, professionally encased in perspex should not adorn an executive office or meeting room for the next hundred years or more, to serve as an inspiration and constant reminder of an earlier idealism.

Of course it takes effort and money, but it is a heritage worth preserving, both as a debt of honour to the pioneers of trade unionism and as a responsibility to the generations of trade unionists yet to be born. Taking a broader and longer view, we need the unashamed commitment of a future Labour government that adequate state funding will be made available for the proper housing, conservation and preservation of all the historic material of the labour movement in the same way that public money is used to support institutions like the Imperial War Museum. In the meantime, we must continue to search and find against the day when labour history is accorded its rightful recognition as the heritage of the British people. Around the country there are still precious banners to be found. Only a few weeks ago I found a hundred glass negatives of Tutill-made union banners, most of which have long been lost or destroyed. The find has come too late for proper evaluation and inclusion in this book, but is further confirmation of the treasures of our working class history still to be revealed. The need to recover our past is crucial in the face of a government that seeks to distort, deny and destroy the history of British trade unionism.

John Gorman
May 1986

INTRODUCTION

GWYN A. WILLIAMS

PRESENTING JOHN GORMAN'S COLLECTION

In the summer of 1831 the workers of Merthyr Tydfil broke into insurrection against the established order. Colliers, miners, some skilled furnacemen, ravaged by slump but innocent of union organisation, they were seized by a vision of social justice at the height of the political crisis over the first Reform Bill. They marched on Merthyr to recapture for the poor those petty properties which had been confiscated by the debtors' court of the shopkeepers. And they marched under banners.

Makeshift banners they were for the most part: white ones inscribed 'Reform'. One young boy, Abednego Jones, carried a flag as big as himself, shouting, 'Death to kings and tyrants! The reign of Justice for ever!' To house after house, over a hundred of them, the banners went, witness to a great ritual of expiation and retribution. Into the great ironworks they went, to summon forth the laggard. John Petherick, a works agent, met a party carrying one out through the gates. 'Here!' said the banner bearer, 'lay your hand on the flagstaff.' Petherick did so. 'Right,' said the bearer, 'you're sworn in.'

To have 'carried a banner' in the Merthyr Riots marked a man for years; it was remembered in court record and obituary. And under a banner, which some said was red, some said was black and some said was just a flag, they marched the next morning to confront the Argyll and Sutherland Highlanders sweltering in from Brecon. Into the gutter the banner went when, after an hour of furious argument, the crowd attacked the soldiers and the soldiers fired and went on firing. As sixteen bodies were recovered by the soldiers, as a dozen more crawled off to die in corners, as scores more huddled over their wounds in frightened and angry kitchens, as newcomers preaching a novel colliers' trade union moved bewildered among insurgent crowds, men by the hundred took to the hills to raid farms and powder shops for weapons and to brace themselves for conflict with the Regulars and the Yeomanry. There was no doubt about the colour of their banner then. At Hirwaun, up on Aberdare Mountain, the rebels ritually sacrificed a calf, washed a flag in its blood and impaled a loaf of bread on the staff. His arms drenched to the elbows, the bearer set off with his bloody talisman of the people's martial law to summon the 'Sons of Vulcan' to insurrection.

Nine years later, nine years of the making and breaking of popular movements in Britain's age of iron, people in Manchester gathered to greet the Chartists Peter McDouall and John Collins on their release from prison. This was Engels's Manchester, shock-city of the new industrial order, the Manchester which had known Peterloo, the struggle for unions, craft, industrial, local and general, political organisation, the campaign for factory reform, for Owenite socialism, for a working class consciousness of themselves and the world. Behind their marshals, Bill Grestley and Josh Ward, resplendent in the green scarves of Chartism, the trades and the Chartists marched the two miles from Stevensons Square to Salford under a forest of banners blazoned with the heraldry of dissidence and assertion.

ORDER OF THE PROCESSION
Two marshals on horseback with green scarfs and
green and white favours
Portrait of Dr McDouall surmounted by the
inscription 'The Tyrant's Foe'
Twenty committeemen with staves, scarfs and
favours

THREE NATIONAL FLAGS
White Flag   Green Flag   White Flag
ROSE   HARP   THISTLE
Splendid banner of the Brown Street Branch (No. 1),
On one side a portrait of Dr McDouall with the
inscription 'P.M. McDouall is our Friend';
on the reverse the motto 'God and our Rights!'
Eight young women dressed in white wearing green
and white favours and carrying four splendid
garlands
The Manchester Female Radical Association
New Foresters' Band
Council of the Dressers and Dyers of Manchester and
Salford with wands

MAGNIFICENT BANNER,
On one side, the Dyers' Arms, surmounted by the
inscription 'The Operative Dressers and Dyers of
Manchester and Salford'
On the reverse, the inscription 'The Prosperity of the
Working Classes is the Foundation of
National Greatness'
Band
Operative Dressers and Dyers six abreast
Grand Banner
On one side the Dyers' Arms with the inscription
'Branch Good Intent'
On the reverse the Royal Arms with V.R. on the top
Various Trades six abreast
Splendid Green Flag,
Inscription 'Liberty and Equality', surmounting the
Rose, Shamrock and Thistle
On the reverse the same device surmounted by
the motto 'Labour, the source of all Wealth'
The Members of the Whittle Street Branch
six abreast
Tricoloured Flag,
Inscription 'The Rights of Man'
Operatives six abreast

LARGE BANNER
On one side a Painting representing the Massacre of
Peterloo
On the reverse on a black ground the inscription
'Murder demands Justice'
Operatives six abreast

SPLENDID BANNER OF THE
WIGAN ASSOCIATION
On one side a full-length figure larger than life of
FEARGUS O'CONNOR, ESQ.
Holding in his hand a scroll with 'The People's
Charter; Wigan District' inscribed thereon. In the
distance is seen Hunt's Monument surmounted with
the Cap of Liberty, with the Tricoloured Flag flying
and on its base the Inscription 'To the memory of
Henry Hunt, Esq.'
The whole surmounted by the words
'O'Connor, Hunt's Successor!'

On the reverse, the British Lion, rampant, is
trampling under foot 'Starvation Bastilles, Debts,
Funds, Jew Jobbers, Aristocracy, Shopocracy, White
Slavery and State Paupers'. A Mitre is seen falling.
The Lion holds in his left Paw a Flaming Dagger,
from which is suspended a Black Scarf with the
inscription 'Down, Down to Hell; and say I sent you
there!' On a scroll over all the words 'Tremble!
Tyrants, Tremble!'
Operatives six abreast

BANNER OF THE MANCHESTER
BOILERMAKERS
On one side the Boiler-Makers' Arms, motto
'Humani Nihil Alienum'
Surmounted by the inscription 'Friendly
Boiler-Makers'
On the reverse a beautiful allegorical representation
of Unity, Benevolence and Concord with the
inscription 'Success to Trade!'
Boiler-Makers six abreast . . .

Bloody and raw to raw and bloody men scrabbling
with guns on coaltips, heavy in dignity and allegory to
men six abreast who knew the value of labour, the
banner was identity and presence. The future lay
with such as the boilermakers. The bright and
brilliant iconography of British Labour already
blazes through Manchester in 1840: the laborious
armorials of the crafts, the beautiful allegorical
representations, the humanist and learned motto
'Unity, benevolence and concord' – and the lion
rampant despatching the Thing to Hell. Come
blinking out of their dark and secret conventicles into
the fitful sunlight of a precarious legality after 1825,
the trade unions, as years and wheels turned, were to
carry through stony streets silken banners as big as
mainsails, charged with symbolism as complex as a
cathedral.
But many of them had to tread the path of the
Merthyr men. For when the Welshmen were beaten
back into their stalls and saw their brother and martyr
Dic Penderyn unjustly hanged, it was to the colliers'
union they turned. The world they then entered was
the world of the secret password, the darkened room
and the blindfold initiation, the naked sword and the
skeletal figure of Death. The heraldry of Labour
emerged from a shadowy half-world of craft memory
and secret solidarity, as under the impact of the new
industry old traditions crumbled and working men
struggled to build community in the face of black and
brittle and at times ubiquitous hostility. It was in these
years that, in characteristically defensive irony, they
took for themselves one of the mocking songs of their
enemies: 'We are John Bull's youngest bastards'.

BEND SINISTER

After paying entrance fees our society had about forty pound to spare and not knowing what better to do with it we engaged Mr Thomas Jones to paint for us a banner emblematical of our trade, with the motto, 'May the manufactures of the sons of St Crispin be trod upon by all the world', at a cost of twenty-five pounds. We also purchased a full set of secret order regalia, surplices, trimmed aprons etc. and a crown and robes for King Crispin.

Thus the shoemakers of Nantwich in 1834, steeped in the twin and overlapping traditions of the artisan guild and the secret society. In the following year, their King rode through town on horseback, attended by train bearers and officers with a Dispensation, a bible, a pair of large gloves and fine specimens of their work, their 'masterpieces', supported by five hundred marching men in neatly trimmed white aprons with a representative 'tramping artisan' in full tramping kit with walking stick bringing up the rear. The year after, in proper ritual, the officers of this flamboyant union were arrested in the general assault on trade unions which reached a grisly climax in the transportation of six Dorchester labourers, the Tolpuddle Martyrs.

The Dorchester men were punished for taking an unlawful oath, and even after legalisation in 1825 unions were often still steeped in the ritual of a 'secret order'. Delegates arrested at Exeter were carrying two wooden axes, two large cutlasses, two masks and two white robes, a large figure of Death with dart and hourglass, a bible and a testament. Colliers and building workers in their houses of call marched as at drill and had pistols fired over their heads as they took the union oath. Among the Yorkshire woolcombers in the 1820s initiation demanded an apparatus of ritual: 'swords, death-scenes, gowns, banners, battle-axes and large empty boxes like military chests'. There were inner and outer tilers, private rooms in pubs were sealed up. In one union in Leeds

When a member is admitted there are two rooms, in one of which the Lodge is assembled. The first operation was to blindfold him; he was then conducted into the Lodge by two members; he was then required to give the pass word, which on that occasion was Alpha and Omega; he was then walked around the room, during which time a great rumbling noise was made by a sheet of iron – a hymn was then sung – and he still continued to walk about the room two or three times, and was asked if his motive was pure – they then took the bandage from his eyes, and the first thing he saw was a picture of death as large as a man, over which was the inscription 'Remember Thy End'. Over this picture there was a drawn sword – his eyes were then bandaged again, and he was

walked about the room when, upon a signal being given, all the members made a great stamping noise with their feet – he was then ordered to kneel down beside a table and the bandage was again taken from his eyes, when he saw a large bible before him, his hand having been placed upon it . . . The ninety-fourth Psalm was then read ('Lord, how long shall the wicked, how long shall the wicked triumph? . . . They break in pieces thy people, O Lord . . . Who will rise up for me against the evil doers? . . .').

Secrecy of course was an operational necessity. As the structure of the trades was disrupted and transformed from the late eighteenth century, as the old paternalist economy crumbled and the stark orthodoxies of political economy and evangelicalism established their hegemony, the clubs of the trades had to fight. Against the wind their banners streamed. Government and established society closed ranks against French Revolution and British *Jacobins*, Luddite rebellion and Peterloo radicals, the counter-economics of the labour theory of value and Owenite cooperative socialism, primitive methodist enthusiasm and the proletarianised enlightenment of infidel zetetic societies and working men's self-education. Common law, master-and-servant precepts, Combination Acts, a generalised and specific hostility weighed like a mountain on these men's harassed and determined brains. Half-outlaw, half-traditionalist, they fashioned the sworn and secretive society as a necessary instrument of struggle.

But it went deeper than that. Their sworn society was to protect and extend their threatened sense of community and identity. As in so many other occult organisations which pullulated in this, Europe's golden age of the secret society, they deployed all the resources of ritual and ceremony towards the enforcement of mutuality and solidarity. The fearsome oath and darkly ominous initiation, tempered by fraternal and alcoholic conviviality, buttressed by any and every sanction men could dredge up from their experience of community, fellowship, popular religion, theatre, carnival, broke a man from a cruel and corrupt society and bound him to his brotherhood. Repeated rituals of affirmation, repeated experience of sharply defined community, strengthened the bond; the practice of mutual self-help sealed it. A world of visual and personally-sensed symbolism encompassed it.

They found warrant in the older artisan trades they grew from or copied, in particular those trades which lived an inheritance, real or imagined, from the old guilds. The country-wide network of often highly organised trade societies was rich in pageantry in the guild style. The Preston 'guilds' in 1802 staged jubilee processions for a week, woolcombers and cotton-workers glowing in colourful symbolism and preceded by 'twenty-four young blooming handsome women, each bearing a branch of the cotton tree'. On the eve of the great Bradford woolcombers' strike of 1825, when fifteen Newcastle 'trades' sent assistance, the men staged their last gorgeous feast of Bishop Blaize, with heralds, artisans on horseback gaily caparisoned, the Bishop himself adorned with shepherds and shepherdesses and followed by 470 woolcombers in wool wigs, 40 dyers in red cockades and a glittering display of craft in carnival. After 1825 their banners were no less resplendent, the London ropemakers with a swarm of bees around a hive – 'Sons of industry! Union gives stength!' or the Thames Shipwrights' Provident Union with their blue silk banner – 'Hearts of oak protect the aged'. It was this proud ceremonial of producers which the trades bequeathed to the unions.

They transmitted a closer, more intimate tradition of self-discipline: the strict administration of benefits, insurance against sickness, unemployment and a pauper funeral, the rigorous rules against swearing, blasphemy, ridicule, improper conduct, against members 'poxed by an unclean woman'. This discipline, too, had its symbolism, its heraldry. Both discipline and symbolism were ingrained in the newer unions.

Clearly the friendly societies were a major channel of transmission. A million strong by 1815, enjoying some favour from authority, flourishing in local autonomy, they ranged from ephemeral goose-clubs and box-clubs to massive national organisations like the Oddfellows. Their public pageantry, from 'fifty women preceded by a solitary fiddler playing a merry tune' to the bands and choirs of sashed and aproned hundreds, rivalled that of the temperance societies and Sunday schools. They talked the language of community, blending Christian precept with Owenite socialism. 'They helped every one his neighbour; and every one said to his brother, be of good courage.' The brotherhood implicit or dormant in Dissent they made explicit and fused with the learned economy of labour the source of all wealth. Through them without doubt came much of the symbolism of Freemasonry and its lodges which they copied. The all-seeing eye of the Masons was to glower from trade union banners right through to 1914 and with it much of the mystery of craft. Through Freemasonry and mutuality percolated the precepts of the radical enlightenment, humanity, reason, the liberal virtues charged with a communal and collectivist meaning.

Working people had created a rich subculture for themselves, dense with institutions, clubs, unions, education societies, cooperatives, chapels. From it the trade unions emerged and from it they drew their imagery: from old craft, Freemasonry, friendly society, temperance group, from the chapel and the Sunday school, from the bible and from Bunyan. After 1825 the unions rapidly abandoned the secret society (though not its insignia). They marched the streets with their banners. Already by 1831 the miners were beginning their career as the greatest banner bearers of them all: at Jarrow they paraded, each colliery with its own. The banners were out in force at political rallies, the Ten Hours Campaign meetings; in 1834 the unions marched against the transportation of the Dorchester men like regiments of guards, strictly marshalled behind thirty-three banners in battle array.

These were the years of great blood-red dreams of brotherhood and the cooperative commonwealth, of the Builders' Guild with its Birmingham Guildhall. Through them and the Chartist times which followed, banners multiplied, often swift *ad hoc* productions, often full of fierce jeering fight. But when the dreams faded and the mushroom unions died, when the slow process of painful construction, town by town and craft by craft, began, from the 1840s, the trade union banner in what became its traditional form emerges. The earliest banner John Gorman has been able to find dates from the 1820s; it is in the 1840s that a recognisable tradition begins, that George Tutill who was to become banner-maker-in-chief to the unions sets to work.

Over two generations of travail and turmoil, in the teeth of back-breaking and heart-breaking resistance, the working classes, against all odds, had established a *presence*. As they began their long climb through industrial society towards emancipation, it was presence they had to proclaim. In trade after trade the first impact of the new order was felt as disruption, disturbance, the overthrow of old and cherished values, old and cherished moralities. In a new and rapidly changing society, inimical to them in spirit and immoral to them in meaning, working men had to establish their value, their worth, their 'respectability', their very presence. As their unions began to harden into some permanence and continuity, as unionism itself stiffened into a 'tradition', so their pageantry and symbolism began to firm and steady into a kind of permanence. Their banners became enterprises of the spirit, large and silken and heavy and expensive; memorials to a certain permanence. And the heraldry first blazoned in this slowly forming tradition was the heraldry of *presence*.

PRESENCE

During the 1840s union banners began to be made in the general style which remained in favour for a hundred years: lavishly illustrated on both sides of silk panels, highly ornamented and trimmed, up to 4.9 by 3.7 metres in size, to be paraded in public, stately and striking. This uniformity, which extended to designs as well as materials, was due largely to one man, George Tutill, who set up in the banner-making business in 1837 and over the next fifty years earned for his business a virtual commercial monopoly and a world-wide market. In 1859 George Tutill moved to a specially designed building at 83 City Road to exploit the high skills and low wages of the East End silkweavers. In July 1861 he took out a patent for his process of coating the silk with india rubber which vastly improved the quality and durability of the banners with their oil paintings. In the 1880s he installed the largest Jacquard loom in the world. John Gorman, who discusses Tutill's work in detail, has made the startling discovery that over 75 per cent of all trade union banners since 1837 were made by this one firm.

Tutill made banners for a wide range of societies, but his speciality was union work. His commercial success was no artificial creation. There was a confluence of union demand and Tutill supply. Tutill's designs were what these anchored and aspiring men wanted. As late as the 1930s, union men were still ordering the cherished late-Victorian public art enshrined in Tutill's massive catalogues of the 1890s. Tutill's measured flexibility, his capacity to produce at a possible price a form of public and popular art which could immediately *communicate* in visual terms at once familiar and elevated and yet leave room for high spirits struck the resonant frequency of union men. The basic forms and modes of banner art were *fixed* in the pudding time of mid-Victorian prosperity to the satisfaction of the labour aristocrats who then staffed the unions; those forms proved equally congenial to successive generations of new unionists at least up to the First World War; such adjustments as were made responded to the general movement of popular public taste, for example in advertising styles of the 1920s. Even when taste had altered drastically, union men in the inter-war years seem to have been very reluctant indeed to move out of what had then become a tradition. It is a striking testimony to the aptness and fitness of George Tutill's designs.

Apt was his decision to open up in City Road in 1859; it coincided with the rise of the London Trades Council and the beginning of a decade which saw trade unionism established as a recognised and respected interest in British society. Even more apt was his decision to install the great Jacquard loom; in 1889 came the massive explosion of the new unionism as British society matured into democracy. In 1889 banners came out of Tutill's at a rate of more than one a day. Most apt of all was his decision at the age of twenty in 1837 to make a commerce out of banners. George Tutill grew with the unions and wove their perspectives into permanence.

Most banners had been produced locally by the neighbouring signwriter, coachmaker, branch member with talent. Hundreds, indeed thousands, of such banners must have been created for temporary or long-term needs and many banners of all kinds continued and continue to be so produced. 'Mother made the first banner the branch had . . .' is a fairly common statement in union folklore. No doubt had more of these banners survived Tutill's pre-dominance would seem far less overwhelming. But

survival is the key. Tutill seems to have sensed the thrust for worth, value, respect and respectability in these men, their need to assert *presence*, no doubt because he felt it himself. What he offered them in his banners was precisely a measure of substance and permanence, a controlled exercise in conspicuous expenditure which would register on the minds they wished to reach. The banners were large-scale enterprises in public declaration, display and advertisement. It was a serious business for a branch to order a Tutill banner; it represented a major commitment. And it became a major aspiration. As unions settled into a certain permanence, a rich banner became a badge of success; there was considerable competition. The increasing number of public displays in galas and demonstrations stengthened the trend. While banners by the hundred were produced all over the country it was the Tutill banners which moved into the mainstream of union heraldry. It was they who established the tradition.

Startling evidence of their success came in the miraculous year of 1889 when with the Great Dock Strike masses of hitherto excluded men, labourers and general workers, poured into the union movement, men of radical temper, radically different in kind from the entrenched union men with their top-hat-and-watch-chain leaders. There was a parallel explosion of new union pageantry. And, inevitably, it came to a focus on Tutill's. There was an orgy of banner making, with solemn unfurling ceremonies and parades, with branch after branch competing with each other for the best display. Tutill's was besieged. For with a Tutill banner, a branch *arrived*.

Tutill's moved and grew with the union movement it served. After the great storms of the 1830s union growth was slow, but careful, measured and irresistible. In the mines and textile enterprises of the North, union development, while intermittent, built up rooted local organisations which began the shuffle towards national unity. The first success was registered among the engineers with the formation of the Amalgamated Society of Engineers under William Allan in 1851, the first of those 'new model' unions the Webbs so admired, with strong benefit funds, the beginnings of a national bureaucracy, the sparing but effective use of the strike, the concentration on skilful bargaining and respectability. Older craft unions reshaped themselves towards this model, and after the big builders' struggle in London in 1859-60 the process intensified. In the 1860s the London and Glasgow Trades Councils stabilized themselves, Robert Applegarth's Amalgamated Carpenters and Joiners followed the engineers; the protection of the 1855 Friendly Societies Act and the relaxation of the legal pressure on picketing fostered further growth.

In the 1860s the unions emerged as a substantial interest anchored in British society. They won middle class support, from positivist intellectuals and the Social Science Association. They were becoming an established pressure group with the beginnings of a national leadership in Allan, Applegarth, Alexander McDonald of the Scottish miners, George Odger of the shoemakers and the maverick George Potter with his paper the *Beehive*. They survived the crisis of the Sheffield outrages of 1866 and the subsequent Royal Commission. Indeed so skilfully did they and their respectable allies handle the Commission that its net effect was to root the unions in society with the grudging assent even of *The Times*. In 1868 the first Trades Union Congress was held; by 1874 the TUC had over 150 affiliated unions with over a million members. Its parliamentary committee was active; the unions moved into the radical campaign for reform of the franchise in the late 1860s and established their characteristic connection with Liberalism. The onset of the Great Depression checked their progress; between 1872 and 1875, while unionism spread to the land and the railways, 320 unions were formed and dissolved. The caution of the amalgamated and the craft unions hardened into a defensive corporatism, and the oncoming generation of radical union leaders and the new socialists railed at them as 'coffin clubs' for cowardly and constipated 'labour aristocrats'. But they had certainly arrived – and their gorgeous Tutill banners proved it.

Lenin was to write scornful analyses of a labour aristocracy parasitic on British imperialism; Marx and Engels spoke of bourgeois England creating not only a bourgeois aristocracy but a bourgeois working class as well. In many ways these 'new model' unionists were in fact more coherently class conscious than their predecessors; at the crunch, their class commitment was apparent – as the occasional sharp and swingeing banner broke the general pattern of resolute 'good intent'. But it was a class consciousness which was essentially corporate, integrated into the system which they largely accepted and tried to work to the benefit of their class. They retained and certainly expressed a sense of their own worth but increasingly they expressed it in terms of a general system of values which could not fail to be 'middle class'. As the last remnants of the visionary Chartist land plan symbolically disappeared into the Abbey National Building Society, the cooperative movement followed a similar path. In the mid-century years of swelling prosperity, sectors of the working classes moved into a certain comfort, in an atmosphere tense with improvement, self-improvement, endeavour and a type of licensed radicalism. Millions festered outside the institutional nation whose liberal–radical sector the unions were penetrating; scores of desperate fighting organisations struggled into a brief life and died. But the established unionists built weighty working class institutions into society. They made their presence visible and in the process created the basic character of labour heraldry.

That heraldry was on display in demonstration after demonstration. During the miners' strike of 1844 in Northumberland and Durham no fewer than seventy-two banners were paraded, most of them silk and beautifully painted; in 1871 the miners marched under banners to the first of the famous Durham Galas. Union banners were out to greet Garibaldi in 1864 and for the Reform meetings of 1866 when at Birmingham 200,000 men marched in a procession two miles long under a score of them. A union banner, 'Unity is strength', is the focus of John Holland's painting *Election Day at Derby*.

Their temper can be caught from a drawing of the demonstration which greeted the release of five cabinetmakers from Coldbaths Field prison in 1875. Sentenced for peaceful picketing, they had been the occasion for a successful union campaign against the law. Two banners of the cabinetmakers are there: 'Unity is strength' and under the blazon Justice, the motto 'We protect those the Law would leave to starve'. Behind is a banner perhaps made for the occasion: 'Injured but not dead', and 'We bide our time'. At the head goes a banner, probably of the coachmakers, with the slogan most popular among unions at this time: 'United to support but not combined to oppress' (page 67). An almost identical motto graces one of the earliest banners John Gorman has found, that of the Liverpool tinplate workers which probably dates from the national organisation of the early 1820s and seems to have been based on a membership card. It is simple, amateur but striking (page 69). A Union Jack in the corner symbolises the national character of the union; the Masonic all-seeing eye looks upon the centrepiece *fasces*, the unbreakable unity of the bundle of sticks, supported by the customary female figures of Justice and Hope.

These themes were central: unity, brotherhood, mutuality, coupled with an assertion of the essentially moral and innocent character of the organisation. They were never servile – 'We bide our time' – but the stress was always on conciliation not conflict. And when they chose to advertise their service as benefit societies (as they did with increasing emphasis) their banners were drenched in the biblical imagery of the Good Samaritan. The mottoes of the 1860s and 1870s speak for themselves: 'Unite in love' (tinplaters), 'Through love and unity we support each other' (sawyers), 'Justice to all men' (ironworkers), 'Industry and benevolence unite us in friendship' (woodworkers), 'Justice to the toiler, but may they [capital and labour] ever be united' (dockers), 'God helps those who help themselves' (several trades), and repeated over and over again, 'Come let us reason together', and 'United to protect not combined to oppress'. The first essential was to establish the dignity and worth of the job. Trade after trade which could (generally by an act of imaginative will!) claim some connection with a medieval guild built the old coats of arms into their union banners. The very earliest banner John Gorman has found is that of the United Tin Plate Workers' Society of 1821, from Liverpool (page 68). It is a direct copy of the armorial bearings of the Worshipful Company which grew from the medieval guild and was incorporated by charter in 1670. The coachmakers of 1834 lifted the arms of the Worshipful Company and blazoned them on their beautiful banners, taking them into the National Union of Vehicle Builders in the twentieth century (page 84). They went one better by adding the Royal coat of arms! The tailors preferred the armorial bearings of the Worshipful Company of Needlemakers and borrowed from them the figures of Adam and Eve as the first people to wear clothes (page 83).

One of the cleverest assumptions of ancient dignity was that of the Cooperative Smiths, of Newcastle. This striking and unusually plain and attractive banner (page 78) displays a raised arm with hammer and over 'A voice from the forge' blazons 'All arts do stand'. This motto is lifted from the Worshipful Company of Blacksmiths: 'By hammer and hand all arts do stand'.

Most characteristic perhaps are the banners of London branches of the Society of Watermen and Lightermen, founded in 1872. They took a regulatory act of 1859 as 'reincorporating' the old Worshipful Company of Watermen, and the latter's coat of arms together with the significant dates of 1514 and 1555 figure on their banners. They also tended to dignify themselves by painting into their banners prominent men who had assisted them. Admiral Bedford Pim and another Tory MP Colonel Hamilton were duly commemorated, while a brilliantly scarlet Cardinal Manning (for his services during the dock strike) glows from another (pages 114 and 115). This assertion of ancient and worthy dignity buttressed by the respectful acknowledge-ment of the patronage of the distinguished ran parallel to a proclamation of belief in conciliation. 'Come let us reason together' called the Durham miners as they painted into the association banner the scene when Mr Roberts secured the cancellation of the yearly bond (page 78). The Ipswich dockers had a delightful scene of two men awaiting the coming of a superb sweeping ship with the 'arms' of Empire around their feet. The all-seeing eye looks out over clasped hands and 'Unity is strength', but on the reverse, under a 'Justice to the toilers', an angel ('May they ever be united') presides over a handshake between a workman and a capitalist, top hat, moneybags and all (page 86).

Underlying this pacific approach ran the basic drive to invest their labour with dignity and worth. Some of the most beautiful banners simply display work. The Hull seamen in 1887, for example, painted superb ships with a Britannia and little cameos on a man's working and family life (page 73). Another very early pre-Tutill banner, the Whitehaven sawyers' of 1836,

presents in stark but effective simplicity a ship, two workmen and the tools of the trade. This graphic presentation of work itself was to become perhaps the single dominant theme of most trade union banners for several generations. Painted with a loving photographic exactitude, they celebrate a craft.

Around this central theme, men wove fancies to express a real or imagined heritage of tradition and respect and worth, sometimes lightly done. It was perhaps inevitable that the tobacconists blazoned Sir Walter Raleigh, and the stonemasons the Temple of Solomon. Preston typographers had a Renaissance Caxton at his press and 'Knowledge is power' (page 75). The fine banner of the Chatham branch of the Woodworkers (page 81) reproduces the emblem designed by the artist A.J. Waudby in 1866 for the celebrated Amalgamated Society of Carpenters. It features Joseph of Nazareth, 'the most distinguished member of the craft on record', with Truth and Justice and a *'Credo sed caveo'* ('I believe but I beware' – a very popular slogan!) On the reverse there is a precise and detailed picture of the centring of an arch drawn from a trade handbook and an interior of a joiner's workshop, all flanked by portraits of two officers of the union.

Parallel to the celebration of the craft ran the celebration of its brotherly virtues. On no subject did the banners lavish such attention as on the provision of insurance against accident, illness and death. This, perhaps the most direct form of self-advertisement, came to dominate most banners. Upon it the designers bent minds attuned to the morality picture and given to cameo sketches of sentiment and sentimentality. When the London Carmen's Trade Union went into the National Union of Vehicle Workers in 1891 its new banner, under 'Unity is strength' and portraits of Justice and Charity, vividly portrayed a street accident, and on the reverse the visit of union officers in sashes to the sickbed: 'I was sick and ye visited me' (Matthew 25:36). Other banners of the same union fill their borders with accidents, the payment of benefits, the comforting of a widow, the winning of a compensation case, just as the miners were wedded to their 'The last good morning' and 'Compensation day' (page 93). Nowhere do the banners seem so Victorian, nowhere were they perhaps more immediately effective.

These basic themes were to remain central to union iconography for generations. And as the union world grew, branch after branch seems to have felt the urge to incorporate all of them into one comprehensive statement. There was a steady movement towards banners of a staggering complexity and totality. A trend towards greater and greater size proved self-defeating but there was an apparently irresistible drive to build up on one single banner a huge and complex structure of pictorial representation of the craft, of its Samaritan functions, its history and traditions and its aspirations, all wreathed in scrolls and laurels and figurative females. It was often literally a structure, for the concept was architectural, a great building or pyramid with niches for symbolism, an informative and often equally symbolic background, all festooned with insignia drawn from a variety of traditions. The effect, in blazing colour, must have been overpowering: assimilation must surely have required time and concentration.

The ironfounders' banner based on their membership certificate of 1857 is a classic instance (page 79), the man hacking at coal, centre, forming the focus for a whole complex of scenes, figures and symbols building up into a massive and complex structure rising from a busy and representative background. The 1888 banner of the Watford branch of the Operative Bricklayers is even more striking (page 85). Centre is a scene of the first bricklayers building the Tower of Babel: 'Every house is builded by some man, but He that built all things is God'. Around it climbs up to Heaven a massive and almost indescribably complex structure, crammed to the limit with medallions, verse, symbols, scenes, figurative virtues, slogans, clasped hands, the eye – almost every symbolical representation of unionism one can think of. And at the corners, like *de voto* offerings, the cameo scenes of accident, sick benefit, superannuation, and a highlighted gravewreath to the founder of the union, William Brightwell.

The parallel is unmistakable. This banner needs to be studied with the same loving care, the same eye for realistic detail and symbolic meaning as a stained-glass window, a sculpted west door or a reredos. What these men were creating was a *cathedral*. It makes a fitting climax to the heraldic assertion of presence in community. The banners had come to proclaim *homo faber*, Man the Maker. On those banners union men raised cathedrals to labour.

The Watford men built theirs in 1888. The very next year the 'full round orb of the dockers' tanner' rose over the horizon. Their cathedrals were about to be invaded by the multitude.

CATHEDRAL AND COMMONALTY

In 1889 Tutill's made more banners in a single year than ever before or since.

In that year thousands of the excluded exploded into trade unionism. Ben Tillett and Tom Mann plunged into the misery of dockland, beginning with tea operatives. The Bryant and May match girls struck in a blaze of publicity. Will Thorne organised the gas workers, with Eleanor Marx on the committee. The resurgent socialism of the 1880s interpenetrated with plebeian revolt to sweep to a climax in the Great Dock Strike of 1889. Day after day dockers marched with

their red rags on poles, their stinking onions and fish heads; week by week the silken banners of union men joined them. At a critical point, Australian brothers came to the rescue – and as bronzed and muscular heroes in bush-hats won a deathless glory in banner iconography. Victory saw a forest of banners dipping in salute.

The docks blazed into colour. The tea operatives had their plain, and now sacred, original sewn on silk to preserve it (with the 'i' in 'strike' left out – page 87). Branches blazoned themselves as centurions, summoned up King John, displayed themselves at work, indulged a buoyant and victorious imagination. Week after week, unfurling ceremonies bright with music enlivened hall and street and as the tidal wave of the 'new unionism' broke across the country, the banners rose. The great Labour May Day of 1890 saw vast crowds in the streets under scores of new banners; the TUC at Liverpool staged a parade which was at once solemn affirmation, street theatre and carnival. May Day 1896 saw £20,000-worth of banners on show. In the 1890s something like a banner mania seized working people and not only in their unions. Banners went everywhere, to meetings, demonstrations, funerals, even picnics; the country broke into a rash of £50 raffles. In the decade 1890-1900 the British people seem to have wantoned in colour.

The first wave of democracy heralded a generation of swift, unhinging change. The imperial economy slithered into its protracted crisis as universal male suffrage, general literacy, a broadening of horizons, a quickening of intellectual and spiritual challenge, a multiplication of white-collar jobs, an upward movement of working people blurring skills and grades, a remorseless advance of innovation, bicycle, union, bus, popular organisation, reshaped society. General unions mushroomed in a spirit of revolt as a more militant, often socialist impulse penetrated the world of labour.

In the 1890s depression struck; employers and law courts moved into counterattack. The new unions slumped, grew conservative, began to assume the pattern of the 'coffin clubs' they had mocked; the latter in self-defence lurched into radicalism. From 1900 they turned towards the new Labour Party, and when the Liberals began to build the welfare state, labour plunged into another spasm of crisis-ridden growth. Ulster, Tories, women rebelled, the TUC swept over the three-million mark, Marxism and revolutionary syndicalism fermented in *Miners' Next Step*, the Scottish and Liverpool struggles, the groping towards a triple alliance of miners, transport men and railway workers. The swell of unrest after 1910 carried working people into the traumatic experience of world war, after which the all-seeing eye vanished from their banners. New and militant symbols replaced it as in acute national crisis, British labour with the miners in the front line fought its grim battles of the 1920s through to the momentary exaltation and shattering defeat of the General Strike of 1926.

Under the first impact of the new unionism the world of banners visibly expanded. The banner was essentially an expression of local, of branch pride and in a' few years of tumultuous growth there was a profusion of new ideas. 'This is a Holy War', proclaimed the militant export branch of the dockers, 'and we shall not cease until all destitution, prostitution and exploitation is swept away' and on their dramatic banner a hero wrestles a serpent amid solidarity slogans. 'Be sure you are right', warns a lifebelt circling a ship, 'then full speed ahead' (page 127). The Woolwich Arsenal engineers train a new gun for the eight-hour day (page 88). The Burslem lodge of the miners in 1893 assert that 'Faith can move mountains' to a striking picture of Abraham about to sacrifice Isaac (page 80). On the other hand the Cleveland steel workers in 1897 produced a most respectful 'Come let us reason together' which was unfurled by the manager's wife herself and never carried in anger, while even the Transport and General Workers of West Ham have their self-justifying worker in an ambiguous stance before the powers (pages 77 and 130). The banner of the Sheet Glass Flatteners, found in St Helens during the Pilkington troubles of 1970 and apparently unused since 1923, was strictly traditional, the parable of the bundle of sticks on one side and on the other a bevy of suitably symbolic ladies grouped around a flaccidly sexy Truth gazing into a mirror (page 82).

The style of these banners is certainly cleaner and less cluttered; it is more accessible to modern taste, has less of the archaic and antique 'charm' of the earlier ones. The difference is illusory. Banner art was no counterculture. Its duty was to communicate with the generality, it employed the media of the commons. It moved with public art, most notably with the poster and advertisement art of the 1920s. It was only when the living connection with working people was broken from the 1920s that banner art became a petrified subculture, a conscious archaism expressing 'tradition' and in due time a collector's item worthy to rank, were it but practicable, with other fashionable Victoriana.

The one area of possible exception centres around the socialist artist Walter Crane and his pre-Raphaelite modes; he seems to have had an impact on design comparable to that of Tutill himself on production. This particular style, however, was equally visible in the posters and advertisements of the period. It is true that the specifically socialist banners of the time were distinctive, Crane's *Pasionarias* jostling a species of heightened muscular realism. But while form and content were admirably matched in these, the distinction lay in the message rather than the medium; they were compelling, but they were not *avant-garde*. No banner could move far from the common discourse.

What there is in them is a notable shift towards realism, or more exactly towards humanity. Figurative females and fancy borders abound, and there are picture parables, but even these tend to express an elevated humankind and generally speaking the cabalistic, the occult, and the obliquely symbolic are shunned. Instead there is a minute concentration on exact representation where work is concerned, on the pictorial charged with sentiment for human predicaments. The objective was clearly direct and unmediated communication, graced with a humanity stretching above itself, occasionally in symbolic but never unnatural form. The moral force derived from the interaction between direct pictorial message, colour and slogan. Socialist banners apart, however, the basic message was little changed. Even the first impression that the 'cathedrals' have disappeared is probably false; they have simply been restyled.

Work for example was celebrated as lovingly as ever, in minute photographic detail often so complex and massive as strongly to suggest the 'cathedrals' without the roodscreen artifice. Some of the most beautiful banners are these: the splendid banner of the Penarth coaltrimmers painted by the Cardiff artist W.E. Britton (who like a good artist painted in his name, good and large – page 161). More striking, the banner of the Hendon branch of the General Workers, descendant of Will Thorne's union, which displays on one side the old motto 'Unity, fidelity, love' and on the other the biplanes of the Royal Flying Corps with the exhortation: 'Fewer unions more unity. Work without guidance means chaos. A careful mixture of the two spells success.' The airborne men of Hendon had their feet on the ground (page 150)! And out of the scores of banners chronicling work with all the near-manic dedication of the medieval stonemason towers the superb 1919 painting by H.J. Finn, RA, for the Iron and Steel Trades, building up the many mansions of their great house (page 162).

Nowhere was tradition more rigorously maintained than in the multitudinous banners advertising benefits. 'Do you hear the children weeping O my Brothers?' demands the Stockton branch of the militant National Union of Railwaymen in 1914 over a cemetery scene of mourning family complete with dog at a gravestone 'Sacred to the memory of a brother' (page 93). The boiler scalers and stoke hold labourers in the 1890s had a near-identical scene without the dog but with a union officer in sash (page 99). 'Bear ye one another's burdens' preached the North Staffordshire miners with a Good Samaritan, angels ministering to the sick and the lion lying down with the lamb (page 98). This style hardly changed at all. It was immeasurably strengthened by the old Victorian device of juxtaposing contrasting pictures in a two-sides-of-the-question form. This could be used to tackle any problem and it became very popular after 1918, particularly in the hands of miners and transport men to support the argument that 'Organisation is security' (page 133).

The hero banners, too, point to a development rather than a displacement of tradition. From the 1900s the banners, particularly those of the miners marching in the vanguard of the labour movement, are a portrait gallery of leaders. Havelock Wilson of the seamen, who appears as a Jolly Jack Tar on the 1880s banner of his union, claimed that his features graced fifty banners at a single Durham Miners' Gala (page 112). With the new militancy from the 1890s the local worthies of an earlier day disappeared or were overpainted, to be replaced by branch officers carefully chosen by committee and increasingly by the national spokesmen of Labour. The Durham Gala became a kind of barometer of popularity: they were all there from early heroes through the fallen angels of Ramsay MacDonald and Philip Snowden to Aneurin Bevan, Manny Shinwell and Harold Wilson, with Keir Hardie, of course, towering over all (page 110).

Ellen Wilkinson, however, and she by name only, was the solitary female to figure in this role of honour. With the exception of some banners of the textile trades and of the more militant groups, real working women never appear. Women as angels, virtues, symbols, ever more often Walter Crane's romantic creatures, throng the scene, but Eve the Worker was an absentee, busy one assumes about her properly traditional kitchen and cradle.

For all the wider range and livelier styles, the banners to which the new democracy marched were largely shaped by tradition. Men refurbished that tradition and carried it through war into the travail of the 1920s.

For new departures one has to look to the minority banners of political commitment, to the standards of socialism.

COMMONWEALTH

It was Walter Crane who shaped the first imagery of socialism among the unions. A disciple of Burne-Jones and a friend of William Morris, he touched the fringe of the pre-Raphaelite world. Converted to socialism around 1884, he joined the Social Democratic Federation and the Hammersmith Socialist League and committed himself and his art to the cause of labour, hope of the world, as so many banners designed in his style proclaimed. In 1885 he painted an 'angel of freedom' which was widely copied. Indeed, Crane's women, romantic, sometimes dynamic, always serene, truthful and upright in flowing, swirling robes, were copied without end. In a union banner he designed for the Electrical Trades Union in 1898, the angel is the centre piece of a lively and unusual tableau of light and liberty (page 89). Nature imitated art and when the Women Workers under the fiery Mary Macarthur unfurled their banner in 1914, a striking

woman in Crane style if not by Crane himself, painted by Toye, challenged male comrades (page 119). Another widely imitated design was Crane's engraving for the great May Day of 1891, 'The Triumph of Labour', a cornucopia rout which was to figure on many banners, not least that of the Plymouth branch of the National Union of General and Municipal Workers (page 135). Tutill's was swift to systematize. A standard Tutill design of the 1890s which remained popular for forty years was that of the Usworth lodge of the miners, derived from Crane – a gorgeous, challenging brunette, vaguely reminiscent of the French Marianne, with her red banner of the emancipation of labour, summoning ordinary folk (they are usually 'folk' in Crane) to the cooperative commonwealth across the Communist Manifesto's 'Workers of the world, unite!' Wholly in the Crane tradition was the yoking of such a woman to the 'Workers' Maypole', with wreaths of complex streamers bearing slogans. The Kensal Green branch of the General Workers, for example, produced a maypole which demanded as much attention as any of the 'cathedral' banners – 'No starving children in the board schools', 'Employers liability, abolition of privilege' – a dozen of them (page 178).

All these styles of Crane's or derived from him appeared and reappeared in banner after banner before 1914, especially among the general unions. Sometimes there were effective variations. The Devonport branch of the Workers' Union had a splendid scene in which a dazzling angel broke the chains of a man's slavery: 'Every bondsman has *within himself* the power to cancel his captivity' (page 179). When slogans were used they were often spiky and personal, and the first pictorial socialism of the unions was in fact steeped in the modes and manners of a William Morris self-recreation in community.

Somewhat unexpectedly, something of this tradition survived the war. Several banners follow the style, particularly among the general unions, with noble women, sometimes wrapped in streamers, leading sons of toil into commonwealth: 'The World is my country, mankind are my brethren'. Tottenham's General Workers had such a lady, swathed in light, education, industrial organisation, political action and real international, beckoning workers to a cooperative commonwealth strongly reminiscent of a garden suburb school with the call, 'Producers of the nation's wealth, UNITE! and have your share of the world' (page 125). In others, the tone was harder. Southend's triumph of labour sees a muscular lad break his chains and trample on the wild boar of capitalism before a Marianne, sword in hand and shield of Justice and Equality on arm (page 124).

A harsher note had been sounded before the war. The Rickmansworth branch of the National Union of Railwaymen in 1913 chained its workers to the iron ball of capitalism, blazoned 'Industrial Action' (unique among banners) and asserted that 'The liberation of the working class is the act of the workers themselves' (page 118) – one of the few direct echoes of revolutionary syndicalism. Even more compelling is the remarkable amateur banner of the Jewish trousermakers, with its dark, dramatic simplicity and its sweat-trade verse (page 122):

> We knew the chains of labour
> From earliest childhood days
> We've toiled in dusty factories
> We've shed our blood and tears
> We're marching towards the morning
> We're struggling comrades all
> Our aims are set on victory
> Our enemies must fall
> With ordered step and flag unfurled
> We'll build a new and better world.

Even harsher were the banners out of the first stormy post-war years. Perhaps the most militant banner ever produced was that of the Walthamstow branch No. 1 of the National Union of General and Municipal Workers. On a building site, a workman takes a blackleg by the throat while his mate wards off the boss with a 'Stand back! This is our fight!' (page 121). Uncompromising in a more traditional style was the 1920s banner of the Southall branch of the Associated Society of Locomotive Engineers, to pay for which drivers had shipped and sold Grimsby fish. On a typical banner with medallions of general secretaries and engines, lined with scrolls listing the union's achievement, a giant worker in a red shirt smashes capitalism to let the trains through, trampling on ledgers and secret reports and sending bosses scurrying: 'The power of unity breaks down the barriers of capitalism' (page 117).

It was the miners who in their bitter post-war struggles gave voice to the most intransigent ideological militancy. The United Mineworkers of Scotland who affiliated to the Red International were sent a bilingual banner by their Russian comrades, perhaps the only British union banner made abroad (page 126). The miners had always been banner-bearers-in-chief and it was in their portrait banners that they expressed themselves. After the 'betrayal' of 1931 many lodges sent back their banners of Ramsay MacDonald to have the traitor's face blotted out; in one the eyes had already been gouged out. They were more positive. Chopwell lodge, Durham, one of the 'Little Moscows' of the coalfields, painted Marx and Lenin alongside Keir Hardie, the Soviet emblem alongside the Labour Party badge, to Walt Whitman's 'We take up the task eternal, the burden and the lesson, pioneers, O pioneers!' (page 107). Jim Larkin himself, founder of the Irish Citizen Army, came over to unfurl the banner and in 1954 it was sent to hang in the Hall of Trade Unions in Moscow.

Wardley lodge, Durham, in the 1920s, another 'Little Moscow', produced what must be, implicitly, the most revolutionary banner yet unfurled by a union. Its only insignia were the hammer and sickle and the red star. Keir Hardie was there, together with A.J. Cook the General Strike leader and George Harvey, 'Wardley's Lenin'. But centre, overshadowing all others, was Lenin himself and in another corner, James Connolly, the Irish socialist who led the Easter Rising and was shot as a traitor, portrayed in his Citizen Army uniform (page 106)!

But with this handful of socialist banners from the 1920s, the militant tradition, indeed the banner tradition itself, runs out.

Only the miners, in effect, keep marching on in this style. The last political banners in John Gorman's collection are a handful from South Wales after the Second World War. 'Peace, forward to socialism' calls Mardy lodge, a Welsh Little Moscow; 'Workers of the world, unite!' from Cefn Coed; 'Forward to socialism' drills the Aberaman miner and '*Ymlaen i Sosialaeth*' a Welsh-speaker in a banner of modern design (page 128).

Both the impulse to produce banners and the public proclamation of socialism upon them fade out rapidly after 1926. Even among miners, the heroes of 1920 Wardley are painted out.

The most heartbreaking picture in this book is that of Wombwell's last walk (page 120). Wombwell branch of the Yorkshire NUM had one of the popular step-series banners; a miner steps from nationalisation through a five-day week and all the other reforms towards the daybreak of socialism. Now in 1969, in the black drapings of death, led by the branch secretary, Roy Hepworth, who lost his leg to the pit, the men wheel the banner for the last time, for after 116 years the colliery closes. As so many others have closed, bringing the greatest tradition of British labour to its own close.

BANNERS FURLED?

The shattering defeat of 1926 threw trade unionism back into a long siege. At Tutill's, banner production dwindled and the break in continuity proved almost fatal. Victory and a Labour government in 1945 brought brief revival. The miners in particular greeted nationalisation with bright, crisp and optimistic designs but perhaps the most notable feature of this Indian summer were the banners raised in county after county by the National Union of Agricultural Workers. In many ways these are aesthetically the most pleasing of them all, with the excellent schematic badge of the union echoed in work motifs on the reverse. Perhaps something of the variety of the old intensely local styles has been lost in standardisation, but little of the old vigour. Dorset have a riveting salute to their Tolpuddle martyr George Loveless – 'We will, we will, we will be free' (page 148) – and the NUAW banners, authentic extensions of tradition, make a brave showing at the annual rally in the martyrs' village (page 148).

With the exception of the miners and the agricultural workers, banner bearing and banner making went into a long decline. Some newer designs were produced: the City branch of the Post Office Engineers carries a modern banner based on traditional pattern (page 173) and in 1956 the Mountain and Molehill group organised to serve the movement. Ken Sprague designed a modern banner for the Foundry Workers, a traditional for the Glasgow Post Office Workers and dramatic insignia for an Electrical Trades Union branch (page 135) but a project for a banner department came to nothing . More remarkable and perhaps symptomatic was the banner painted in 1953 for the London Cooperative branch of the Union of Shop, Distributive and Allied Workers; made by Herbert Sharpe, a former Tutill's man, this is so traditional that at first glance it seems a throwback to fifty years ago (page 166).

This choice recalls Tutill's 1930 catalogue with its 1890 styles, the freezing of the craft in the 1920s, the deliberate decisions since then in favour of the old designs apparently *because* they were archaic. This suggests a rather self-conscious identification with a past which is patently remote. Were they smaller, one suspects that in some quarters trade union banners could become as fashionable as commemorative mugs and plates.

The General Strike was clearly a watershed. Time after time on his quest, John Gorman discovered that it was in the 1920s that an old neglected banner had last seen the air. Certainly the thirties were no time for silken banners, but one notes that already in the twenties, there was a certain antiquarianism about many designs. One notices, too, that the banners have flourished at moments of *breakthrough*: even the efflorescence among miners and rural workers after 1945 can be interpreted in such terms. John Gorman estimates that some 10,000 banners were produced between 1832 and 1939. Of the relatively few which have survived, the miners provide the majority, over 250 of them, testimony to their long service in the vanguard. The rest come mainly from those general unions which ultimately coalesced into the Transport and General Workers and the General and Municipal Workers and they date from the explosions of the 1890s and the 1910-26 period.

They served a necessary function in their day and the check in 1926 of course coincided with important shifts in public style and taste. The continuing expansion of print and all manner of aural and visual communication, the rapid changes in taste and fashion, the long erosion until very recently of working class consciousness, the blurring of social and political values and purposes, were all inimical. And in a trade union movement which was a national institution, which scored tactical successes and which counted ten million adherents, the banners shrank. May Day 1898, which had seen 400 of them on show, in 1967 saw 10. The Durham Gala remains a major occasion for display but that, too, shrinks as pits close.

In 1967, for the first time in its history, no trade union banner came out of Tutill's.

In 1967, too, John Gorman was moved to begin his search. In many sectors of popular culture, as Orwell's study of boys' papers and seaside postcards revealed, a single individual properly attuned can work wonders. In the banner world there was Tutill and to a lesser extent Crane; in the black year of 1967 there was Gorman. He comes straight out of a tradition. His grandfather, a South Shields boy, went down Whitburn pit at thirteen and was an active miners' union man until he was thrown out in 1930; his mother was servant to a colliery manager. On Gala Day, while grandfather buckled on the banner straps, the family marched in Durham. His father, a Londoner, carpenter son of a carpenter father, was an ASW man. John himself, trained as a silk-screen printer in Tutill's West Ham, became an art printer, worked with Mountain and Molehill and was active in left-wing and union movements. It was in 1967 that he scrambled over coke in the basement of the West Ham Transport and General Workers' office, humped boxes through a lavatory and up stairs, peeled away the 1926 copies of the *Record*, stroked with the turps and linseed oil and found himself staring at a Cardinal. From that moment, his passion became a crusade. One consequence has been a quickening of interest among trade unionists; another is this book.

Now we have remembered these banners and found many of them again, what are we to do with them? Lock them away in brightly-coloured book and dusty museum? Roll them out on occasion for rituals of ancestor worship? The times of tension have come again and will come, again and again. At the great TUC rally against the Industrial Relations Act, amid a host of placards and posters, sixty of the old banners raised their proud unwonted heads.

This is a time which cherishes heraldry; we are drenched in it. True, the style is not, or not yet, that of the cathedral banner, but Walter Crane is no longer a stranger. We are certainly back with the cabalistic sign. In some ways, the old Masonic insignia of the order of union are against warp and woof of the texture of experience. Certainly, one remembers the racing of the blood when the banner of Penrhiwceiber lodge floated down until it filled the television screen or when the engineers marched to the miners' picket lines at Saltley, crying aloud for *Hold the Fort* and union banners waving high.

INTRODUCTION TO THE NEW EDITION

I wrote those words in 1973. Today, after a dozen years and more, in this new edition of his book, John Gorman can add a new clutch of banners to his collection.

In truth, it has been struggle which has generated them. In 1980, during their national strike, the steelworkers found that their old banner, unused for years, was too fragile to carry. In desperate haste, and at minimal cost, Bryan Blumer of Corby Community Arts painted a new one for them. Intended as a temporary measure, it stands here as one of the most grimly powerful banners in the entire collection (page 186).

Time after time, among these newer banners, you will find that it was some critical event, some often dramatic happening, which drove men and women to make them. And, in making them, it is tradition they refer to. The skills are often new, so are the materials. These have been produced by a wider range of makers, from talented union members to sympathetic artists and art teachers like Sonya Walters, Andrew Turner, Catriona Christison, from suppliers who have become almost 'traditional', like Turtle and Pearce, who succeeded the ubiquitous Tutill's, and the innovative Ken Sprague, to a family group like the Campbells and the people of Chippenham Designs. But all of them fuse the past and present of their unions in a striking and often highly self-conscious manner.

It is a Turtle and Pearce banner, for example, which is the first to blazon a silicon chip, for the Birmingham engineers of the Transport and General Workers (page 188). Alongside the chip, however, borne in honour through all the great 'days' of the trade union movement, stand a motto and a verse in strictly traditional style.

Ken Sprague and his sister Pat Meaden designed a banner for NALGO between 1977 and 1980. It took three years of hard work on twenty-eight vibrant fabrics chosen by Pat and is resolutely modern and innovative in design. But where do the themes come from? From four symbols drawn from the old badge of the union, with the flower symbols of the nations of Britain, the cornucopia of old replaced by a fruit tree of life – with its small but friendly worm at work – to show 'nothing's perfect'! This is, in fact, a 'cathedral banner' for our times (page 187).

The Hosiery Workers (page 187) incorporate the whole history of their union, while the Scots of Lanarkshire follow tradition by blazoning Robert Owen and John MacLean (page 189).

A classic instance is the banner of the West London District of the engineers of the AUEW (page 189). Sonya Walters painted it in acrylic colours on cotton duck canvas. She had already painted a banner for

the Cuban workers killed during the American invasion of Grenada. Her design is strictly contemporary, but it draws on the old tradition of depicting work itself. Within the cogs figure a black toolmaker and a woman engineer. Concorde flies alongside the Asian women who won the Trico struggle. But the motto is the old one – 'Educate, organise, control'!

From time to time, the old flash and fire of the traditional banners flare up. The TGWU clerical workers in Parliament cockily raise a Red Flag over the House of Lords, set Big Ben at a nuclear five minutes to midnight and slap the symbol of the Women's Movement on the back (page 188).

Some of the old internal fires rage, too! When Andrew Turner painted a banner for the Manchester branch of the General and Municipal Workers in 1978-79, he worked closely with the representatives of a militant 2,000 and unveiled it before 200 critical shop stewards. They didn't like his background colour of blue – too 'conservative'. He won the day there, but he had to drop his quotation from Marx – too 'communist' – and replace it with a more mellow sentence from Engels. All, however, were bowled over by his overpoweringly titanic figure of a worker smashing his chains – and the banner has gone down in local legend as 'The Incredible Hulk' (page 186)!

It is less the humour of the banners which grips the mind, these days, than the poignancy of many of them. So many of the struggles, however heroic, have been losing struggles. How can anyone not sense the painful irony of the *Sun* Machine chapel banner here (page 185)? Made by Turtle and Pearce in 1979, at the prompting of two union officials, this SOGAT banner keeps the old NATSOPA blazon out of pride and, at what was then the Fleet Street heart of Rupert Murdoch's empire, they unveiled it to the membership at a dinner to celebrate ten years of the *Sun*, held in the ballroom of the Hilton Hotel!

Inevitably, it is the miners' banners produced in the heat of their desperate struggle of 1984-85 which clutch at the throat. The banner of Goldthorpe lodge, Yorkshire, blazons the strike committee with clenched fists and a 'No Surrender', as miners drive off rats with the faces of Margaret Thatcher, Ian Macgregor, Peter Walker, a judge and a policeman (page 190). In Leicestershire, only thirty men out of 2,400 stuck by the NUM and its strike. Dismissed as 'The Dirty Thirty', they proudly adopted the jeer as a title (a very traditional practice, that!). Chippenham Designs made their badges into a banner, bearing much of the cost themselves. And there they are, Dirty Thirty, clenched fist and no surrender – a banner they carried at the Durham Gala and at demonstrations innumerable (page 190).

It is on an ambiguous note, then, that we must close. It seems all too appropriate that the *Sun* chapel banner was used mainly at functions to mark the retirement of long-serving members, while the Dirty Thirty miners' banner has passed to the worker-historian Dave Douglas on its way to a museum.

In struggle were the banners born, in struggle will they live – and it is going to be a struggle *to* live.

Banners of some kind there will always be. Banners of the kind John Gorman has chronicled may rarely be made again. They are still the visual memory of a movement. For movements, as for men and women, memory, the organised memory which is history, is the only human force which can conquer change and defeat death.

We are going to need those memories, for many of us, literally or metaphorically, will need to go marching yet behind the banner of the lodge into a stony square.

Gwyn A. Williams
Emeritus Professor of History, Cardiff University
May 1986

BANNER BRIGHT

THE LOST BANNERS

At the May Day march in London in 1896 it was claimed that £20,000-worth of trade union banners were carried. They were brilliant, silken sails of colour, up to 4.90 by 3.70 metres in size, painted with emblems and scenes showing the crafts and skills of the trade unionists who carried them. Some of the banners illustrated the hazards and dangers of the work in certain industries – a builder toppling from high scaffolding, a railway worker crushed between two trucks. Others painted a romantic vision of a better life to be gained by 'Unity' and 'Reason not force'. The peak period for banner carrying was undoubtedly the last decade of the nineteenth century when the enormous demand for banners from every sort of organisation, from Sunday schools to trade unions, amounted almost to a mania. Engravings, drawings, photographs and contemporary accounts confirm the vast numbers of ornate silk banners that would be paraded on every possible occasion during this time. In 1890 a newspaper reported 400 banners at a temperance society march in London!

Accounts of the first Labour May Day demonstration, held in London on 4 May 1890, give some idea of the thousands of people there and the number and variety of banners which were carried. The *People's Press*, a trade union newspaper of the time, gave details of assembly points in all quarters of the capital. As the marchers made their way to the embankment, they were joined by trade unionists and supporters waiting *en route* at another twenty assembly points. Of the march itself, an eyewitness described the scene.

High over their heads along the whole line waved gay and brightly coloured banners bearing well executed and bold pictorial devices and suitable mottoes. Each banner was followed by representative men of the various organisations of trades and industries headed by marshalls wearing decorated sashes.

It must have seemed that the whole of organised labour in London was on the move.

Tailors were in great numerical strength and presented by force of contrast one of the most remarkable sections of the assembly. Men from West End shops appeared in black frock coats of modern cut with fresh flower in button hole and tall hats. Behind them, headed by the banner of the Ladies' Tailors' Union with the strange device of a stag of magnificent head jumping a fence, came a tatterdemalion crew of sweated men from the East End.

The United Society of Farriers, 'aristocrats of labour', made their part of the procession

conspicuous by floating above it a huge silk banner upon which was depicted silver horses rampant and the text 'United to support but not combined to injure'. Twenty-five of them rode right gallantly mounted on sprightly steeds, bedecked with saddle-cloths and trappings. They wore blue and white sashes and rode at the head of the procession smoking cigars.

From every part of London they came: the Amalgamated Society of the Sailmakers of the Port of London, their banner painted on a huge sail; gas stokers whose banner depicted the manner in which the men worked in the heat of the retort house, the marchers carrying their shovels and heavy hammers; postmen, their banner declaring 'Each for all and all for each'; engineers from Woolwich Arsenal on whose banner had been painted a 'new gun' firing an eight-hours shot in the direction of the Houses of Parliament; the Dockers' Union, Horse Hair and Fibre Workers' Union, London Carmen's Trade Union, Spitalfields Market Porters' Union, Umbrella Makers' and Mounters' Union, Coach, Bus and Van Union, Stick and Cane Dressers' Society, United Cap Makers' Society, Hebrew Cabinet Makers' Society, House Painters' and Decorators' Union, Stone Masons and Paviors, Clickers' Union, Navvies' Union, Portmanteau and Trunk Makers, East End Ropemakers, Barge Builders, Skinners, Tanners and Curriers, Operative Bakers and Confectioners, Saddle and Harness Makers, the Women's Union, Coal Porters, Carpenters, Printers and Boxmakers. They, and countless other societies and unions, all marched for the Eight-Hour Day and every society had a silk banner.

In Hyde Park fifteen platforms were set up in a huge semi-circle from which 100 speakers addressed the throng. Speaker after speaker told of the hundreds of thousands of workers forced to toil from sixty to ninety hours a week. Among the speakers were Tom Mann, Ben Tillett, John Burns, Will Thorne, Cunninghame Graham, MP, and Eleanor Marx. Exactly how many took part in the demonstration is impossible to verify. H.M. Hyndman writing in *Justice* put the figure at 350,000. The *People's Press* claimed 300,000 while the *Daily Chronicle*, devoting five unbroken columns to the event, put the number at 100,000. Whatever the figure, Engels, who was on the number one platform, said that for the first time in forty years he had heard the 'unmistakable voice of the English proletariat'.

Where, then, are the 10,000 banners which I estimate were made from the time of the first reform bill in 1832, until the beginning of the Second World War? The sad fact is that most have been destroyed. Some are simply lost. Amalgamations of the numerous local trade societies into larger unions, the failure of many small societies to survive at all, the social changes of the last forty-five years, the natural ravages of time and the unnatural ravages of the Nazi blitz, have all taken their toll.

The remainder of these valuable relics, the pictorial record of more than a century of working class struggle were consigned to lie for the most part in cellars and basements, gathering mildew or simply turning to dust in boiler rooms, attics and obscure corners of trade union halls and clubs. Others remain in lofts or garages of long since dead branch secretaries and not a few must still remain, undisturbed, in the pubs where unions once met. It is impossible to be accurate, but it is doubtful if as many as a tenth of the banners are extant. Despite the upsurge of interest in the visual history of the labour movement during the past decade or so, some banners are still being destroyed or neglected and hundreds are yet to be found.

It was the memory of childhood stories of miners' galas and my own experience of trade unionism which made me wonder what had become of the banners once so proudly carried through the villages, towns and cities of Victorian and Edwardian Britain. My search began in 1967, and brought an immediate discovery which was to confirm my belief in the value of the banners as historical relics and to corroborate my fears as to their neglect.

I had heard from two former dockers, J. Green and J. Butcher, that there were old banners at the West Ham office of the Transport and General Workers' Union. The banners were kept in the basement which also housed the boiler and to get there it was necessary to pass through a white-tiled gents' lavatory. We manhandled the dirty and heavy boxes up the stairs where they were loaded onto a lorry and taken to my studio for inspection and photography. The first box contained a banner wrapped in mildewed canvas sheets, while the box itself was lined with yellowed copies of the *Record*, the official organ of the TGWU, dated 1926. I unrolled the banner on the floor of the studio but it was difficult to discern the nature of the design since it was covered with a patina, a milky film produced by a combination of dirt, time and the effect on the colours of the patent rubber process used to give flexibility to the painting. I began to clean the banner with a solution of turps and linseed oil. It was like the restoration of an old oil painting as colours and form began to emerge. The picture was of a cardinal in scarlet robes and skull cap, the last subject I had expected to find on a trade union banner. The next day proved even more of a revelation, for after hours of cleaning the reward was the discovery of an admiral in full-dress uniform.

These first banners yielded a scrap of information that was to prove invaluable in tracing the background to the creation of these huge pictures of the past. Three of the colours were inscribed with the name of George Tutill, manufacturer of patent banners, a name to recur continually during the checking of hundreds of banners over the next four years.

The circumstances of the first discovery set the pattern of many future finds. The next banner to be found was that of the London Jewish Bakers' Union, which was kept in the basement of the Hackney office of the union. Like most of the basements I visited, it was dark and filthy. The box lay on the floor and was almost as long as the room, its centre beneath a leaking sink which had dripped water onto the lid for years. I took hold of the lid, which was a horrible slimy pulp, and my fingers went into it as though it were *papier mâché*. Fortunately, the banner was protected by a waterproof sheet and, although covered in mildew, the banner proved to be in fine condition. I was told by the secretary, Miss Brooks, that the banner had not been out of its box for forty years.

The banner of the Tea Operatives' and General Labourers' Associaton, the original banner of the Great Dock Strike of 1889 and a priceless relic of trade union history, was also found in a basement. The caretaker told me that if I did not want it it would go in the boiler since it had been 'a bloody nuisance for years'.

As the word spread, help came from different parts of the country. Old trade unionists wrote to tell of banners tucked away in branch halls, homes and Labour Party rooms. A union official found the banner of the Ipswich Dockers' Union in the local Labour Party hall. A 1920 banner of the Building Workers was found behind the settee in the front room of the home of a retired branch secretary where it had been for twenty-five years. The banner of the Sheet Glass Flatteners was unearthed by strikers during the Pilkington dispute when they were in conflict with their own union, the General and Municipal Workers. A journey to Bristol to photograph an old banner of the Bakers' Union resulted in another basement discovery, the magnificent banner of the Amalgamated Society of Operative House and Ship Painters and Decorators. Location is a laborious process of appeal to individual branches and pursuit of every rumour, reference or story. After the National Union of Public Employees had drawn a blank in looking for one of their banners, a press photograph appeared in the 'dirty jobs' dispute of 1970 which showed a glimpse of just what I was looking for. Immediately checking where the picture had been taken, I found that the banner belonged to the Bermondsey branch. Made in the 1920s, it had recently been found after being lost for ten years. It showed scenes of the 'means test' and the 'council lock-out' of the thirties. Appeals aimed at branch level brought encouraging results and often unearthed banners which astounded district and national offices. From time to time, stories were told of the oldest trade union banner in Britain, believed to be in Liverpool. Eventually, after a fruitless appeal in the journal of the union in question, the 1821 banner of the United Tin Plate Workers was found in 1970, wrapped in a blackout curtain, in the offices of the National Union of Sheet Metal Workers and Coppersmiths in Liverpool. Old trade unionists frequently told of banners that were there 'the last time we carried it'. This usually turned out to be 1926 and was spoken of as if it were yesterday. It was scarcely surprising that few of these could be found. Not every enquiry was successful. I hunted in vain for the banner of the National Union of Police and Prison Officers, a search which defeated even the detectives of Scotland Yard.

Amalgamations and moves to new offices are times of peril for old banners. When the Woodworkers' and the Painters' Union amalgamated, a district official of the Amalgamated Society of Painters and Decorators paid the local council £4.50 to remove the old banners which he considered of no further use. The banner of the Philanthropic Society of Journeymen Coopers was destroyed when the union moved to new offices. The Amalgamated Society of Coopers lost their historic banner in a fire at the beginning of the century and the Amalgamated Society of Woodcutting Machinists suspect that their old banner was burnt, though there are conflicting stories. The banner of the United Society of Brushmakers, made in 1832 and carried to Newhall Hill at a great reform meeting, was destroyed by fire in 1880 when the 'pan-shop' where it was kept was burned to the ground. Unhappily the decision to order a new banner has often resulted in the destruction of the older and more important banner, as in the case of the Kidderminster Carpet Weavers. A remarkable story is that of the Scottish Union of Power-Loom Overlookers who wrote to say that the theft of their banner remained an unsolved mystery! After pressing enquiries, union organisers frequently admitted to having disposed of or destroyed banners since the end of the Second World War. November 5 appeared to be the most popular date for disposal! The explanations offered were generally that the banner had lain unused and decaying since pre-war and was eventually got rid of as being of no interest, use or value, a not unreasonable conclusion in the circumstances. I thought originally that the old craft unions would have produced the most fruitful yield of banners, but unfortunately very few of these older examples appear to have survived. Banners made before the 1860s are very scarce indeed. Little has been found of the innumerable quaintly-named local craft societies which mushroomed in the nineteenth century, like the Hebrew Cigar Makers, the Bolton Calico Printers or the East End Ropemakers. Some, like the Oldham and District Weavers' Winders and Cord Cutters Association remain only as a print in a banner maker's catalogue. Virtually every society, no matter how small, possessed a banner which was as vital to them as their set of rules. Few unions formed before 1926 did not have a national banner and most had a banner for every branch or lodge. Even the first of the 'white collar' unions, the National Union of Clerks, had banners well before 1914. The big surprise to me, as a former member, was that my old union, the Sign and Display Trades Union, never possessed a banner of their own!.

The question of why some banners survive and others are lost and destroyed has no positive answer. Not all the banners are neglected. Some are treasured like family heirlooms and never taken from their boxes except to show to the curious visitor. Other branches have a pride for their banner which has been passed down the years. In these cases, banners are regarded as a direct link with the pioneers of the union. For some, the banner is still the battle standard to be carried in every struggle, and a hard core is repeatedly seen at demonstrations over the years. Probably the greatest enemy of the banner is high wind. For if the banner is held wrongly, the strong silk can split in a second beyond reasonable repair. Rain, too, is no friend of the banners, causing them to mildew and rot if packed away when wet. Others have been lost in action; a 3.60 by 3 metres banner is a cumbersome burden in the heart of a milling crowd of protestors. On such occasions the police seem to regard a banner as a rallying point to be put down as quickly as possible. It was police action which badly damaged the banner of the Nine Elms branch of the National Union of Railwaymen in 1926, when they broke up a demonstration of strikers. The police arrived in a Carter Patterson van encircled with barbed wire which ripped the banner apart.

However, the banners were safe from every peril except fire if properly stored in the boxes supplied by their original maker. The wooden cases he made to house the banner, poles and straps were up to 4.30 metres in length and weighed almost 25 kilogrammes. Banners stored in these boxes have emerged as good as new after remaining in them for fifty years. The sheer size and weight of the boxes has also made a substantial contribution to the survival of so many banners. It may be an easy job to dispose of a piece of tasselled silk, but it requires serious and considered effort to remove such a box.

My task then has been to make a contribution to the preservation and recording of a single and particularly vivid source of British trade union history, an extant and unique record of 150 years of trade union development and working class progress. Unrecognised and uncharted, it is an exciting and living history, painted in oils and woven in the silk of the thousand banners, the traditional banners of the trade unions.

Unfortunately, it is a source that until recent years was neglected by historians and by the custodians of this heritage, the trade unions themselves. This is a generalisation, but it is fundamentally true, a conclusion reached over a period of four years' field research from 1967 to 1971 and reinforced by further experience and inquiry since then. The trade unions have kept no records concerning the location and condition of their banners. Neither the TUC nor any individual unions have a catalogue listing their banners. Only Ian MacDougall, the dedicated secretary of the Scottish Labour History Society, has attempted to catalogue Scottish trade union banners. Most unions have no idea of the whereabouts of these valuable relics of their own history. Sadly, two important banners unearthed during my original research, those of the London Trousers Makers and the Manchester No. 13 branch of the National Union of Railwaymen, both exhibited at the Whitechapel Art Gallery *Banner Bright* exhibition in 1973, have subsequently been lost again! Despite the development of interest in the visual history of the labour movement and strenuous efforts by the National Museum of Labour History, Labour History Societies and some individual unions like the Transport and General Workers' Union, the National Union of Mineworkers and the General and Municipal, Boilermakers' and Allied Trades Union, there is no overall plan or policy for halting the steady deterioration and, in many cases, actual disintegration of the banners.

In fairness to the unions the lack of central records can be partly explained by the essential democratic structure of the trade unions and the degree of autonomy of the local branches. It is doubtful if a lodge or branch has ever had to obtain national executive permission to purchase the banner or to have given any formal notification to head office that they may have done so. In consequence the existence and location of a banner is usually a matter of local knowledge alone. But the widespread disregard of trade unionists at all levels for the value of their old documents, minutes, mementoes and regalia is almost beyond belief. Since 1945 amalgamations and the moves to new offices and buildings have been the occasion for the dumping and destruction of irreplaceable historic material of all kinds on an immense scale.

An enormous amount has been written on trade unionism; politicians, economists, sociologists, historians and trade unionists have all contributed to the analysis and history of the movement. Indeed, many trade unions have commissioned an official history of their own society or association. These are well researched, well produced and often scholarly works by distinguished academics. There is, however, a common myopia with regard to the visual past that still survives. Very few make more than a passing reference to the banners of the union or unions on which they are writing. Even fewer have seen any advantage in using them to illustrate or corroborate their work. None can be said to have seen in the banners any significant historical value. Yet I would submit that the banners are a field of profitable research to the student of labour history. Like all art, especially commercial art, the banners reflect something of the period in which they were painted. They are grass-roots evidence of the ideals and aspirations of the labouring poor and the organised working class at the specific periods for which they were made. They substantiate and sometimes seem to contradict written history.

It has been necessary to restrict this survey to the official banners of the trade unions. Even then, I have not included the 494 trades councils that exist throughout the country (though they could legitimately be included) due to the sheer size of the task. I commend this as an area of research of visual material worthy of a study in its own right.

The temptation in searching for early material to include the Chartists, the Social Democratic Federation, friendly societies and others was great, but had to be resisted as beyond the purpose of this book. Reluctantly too, the affiliated and allied working class movements, groups such as Labour Party branches, cooperatives, the Communist Party, International Brigade, unofficial liaison committees and many others are excluded. Likewise the slogan banners, which so often epitomize the wit and humour of the British worker during the grimmest struggles. During my searches I have contacted every union affiliated to the TUC and uncovered so many banners it has not been possible to include them all. In selecting the final material, the problem has been what to omit.

I have tried to represent fairly the various crafts, skills and areas of working life represented by organised labour. Also, I have tried to cover the period from the earliest trade union banner I could trace, the tinplate workers' banner of 1821, until 1985. The decision as to how to group the collective material was difficult. Chronological order was impractical due mainly to the sad fact that so few of the thousands of banners made before 1880 have survived. As I surveyed the photographs of the banners a natural grouping emerged. There are the early banners with their mottoes of conciliation, the banners of the 'coffin club' unions with their picture of sickbeds and gravesides, the militant anti-capitalist banners which followed the inspiration of the Russian revolution and the banners that paint the peculiarly British Owenite dream of a cooperative commonwealth. We have glimpses of the pioneers of trade unionism, posed before the plate camera to record their banners for posterity. There are the banners that show the pits and factories where the unionists worked, the tools they used and the products of their labours of which they were justly proud. There are the portraits of the leaders of the men, heroes of their time, and perhaps less exciting but equally relevant are the banners with simple devices of badges and mottoes. Together, the photographs make up a picture of a century and a half of trade union development. A visual grouping seems reasonable for a visual subject and leaves the viewer free to connect the images with his or her own experience and knowledge of trade unionism.

The first edition of *Banner Bright* in 1973 resulted in an awakening of concern for the preservation of union banners and many unions and historians have worked to find and save them for posterity. Good, for it is to the advantage of all trade unionists that the banners should be saved from oblivion and once again be revealed as part of our cultural heritage, a witness to the dignity and courage of our parents and grandparents who fought for justice and a decent life for ordinary working people.

THE BANNERS UNFURLED

Coats of arms were in use throughout Europe by the thirteenth century. Experts differ as to their origin: they probably first appeared on shields, though some favour the tabard, the banner or, in a less martial context, the seals of noble ladies. What is certain is that the devices were originally for the practical purpose of immediate visual recognition. The leaders required a picture standard behind which their followers could muster. That tradition has developed into the science of heraldry, governed by strict and intricate rules translated into what amount to a special language, the technical vocabulary of the College of Arms.

There is no need to consider the protocol of the 'right to bear arms' so far as the trade unions are concerned. Coats of arms or designs which appear to be armorial bearings on trade union banners derive from only two sources: the accredited arms of the craft guilds and the fertile imagination of the banner-painter or emblem-designer making free use of the heraldic art.

To identify themselves, the unions turned first to the symbols and insignia of their trades, the familiar arms of the medieval guilds. The craft guilds were composed of master craftsmen and journeymen who were combined together for mutual protection of the trade and for the common good of the members. They were to be found not only in the cities, but in every important town throughout the land. In the small workshops where masters often worked at the bench alongside the men, the guild was a vital part of the life of employer and employee alike, embracing every aspect of a man's working career. They regulated entry into the craft, determined piece-rates and could even control prices of manufactured articles. From apprentice to master craftsman the guild represented the total interests of its members. With the development of industrial capitalism at the beginning of the nineteenth century, the rapid growth of cities, increasing use of machinery and specialisation in manufacture, the interests of journeymen and masters began to diverge. In the words of Sidney and Beatrice Webb, the guilds became 'cliques of middle-class capitalists' and the journeymen began to form their own trade clubs and unions. They needed to look after their own interests which were no longer parallel with the aspirations of the masters who owned the means of production. In most cases, the means of production now meant considerably more than the craftsman's set of tools.

It is apparent that the journeymen saw themselves as the heirs to the tradition of the crafts of which they were rightly proud, and had no compunction in adapting the armorial bearings of the guilds for their own purpose. Combined to protect their craft interests, tinsmiths, carpenters, paviors, plasterers, painters, farriers, coachmakers, blacksmiths and doubtless many others appropriated the devices and mottoes of the guilds which were so easily recognisable to the union members.

The earliest authenticated trade union banner found during my researches is that of the United Tin Plate Workers' Society made in 1821, when autonomous local tinplate workers' societies from Liverpool, London and Glasgow came together to form a national organisation to 'save the trade'. The date of the banner is confirmed by a receipt found in the old Liverpool society's box, 'To William Dixon for painting and washing etc. a Colour £0. 5s. 0d.' dated 21 July 1821. The banner bears a form of the armorial bearings of the Worshipful Company of Tin Plate Workers, alias Wireworkers, and a direct translation of the Latin motto of the guild, 'Unite in love'.

The Webbs, in their *History of Trade Unionism*, writing on the 'assumed connection between the trade unions and the guilds in Dublin', refer to the use of guild arms and dates on union banners.

> The trade unions not only in many cases bear the same arms as the old guild, but often also the date of their incorporation. Thus, the old society of 'regular' carpenters claims to date from 1490; the regular Operative Housepainters' Trade Union connects itself with the guild of St. Luke (1670) and the local Union of Brick Layers and Plasterers assume the date of the incorporation of the Bricklayers' and Plasterers' Company by Charles II. The Dublin painters now inscribe 1670 on their new banner but the earliest traditions of the members date only from 1820.

The Webbs continue to tell of 'adoption of mottoes, saints and dates of origin of the old Dublin guilds by the unions' and ascribe the motive as

> more interesting as a trait of Irish character than any proof of historic continuity. In short the Irish trade-unionist with his love of the picturesque has steadily annexed antiquity and embraced every opportunity for transferring the origin of his society a few generations further back.

In essence this is true, but the trait is not confined to the Irish. The banners of the Greenwich lodge and the Cardinal Manning lodge of the old Amalgamated Society of Watermen and Lightermen both carry the guild arms of the Worshipful Company of Watermen and Lightermen and a version of the guild motto 'At commaundement of owre superiors'. The banner of the Manning lodge bears two dates, 1514 and 1859. The first date refers to the year of the first Act of Parliament to regulate fares upon the Thames and even pre-dates the establishment of the Worshipful Company of Watermen in 1555. No mention is made on the banners of the date of the founding of the union in 1872 or its short-lived predecessor, the Watermen's and Lightermen's Protection Association of 1866. The union, like the Dublin unions, sought to give the impression of an ancient history and used the earliest dates associated with the guild to achieve this end.

Many other craft unions appropriated guild arms as a means of ready trade identity. In 1896 there is a reference to the Amalgamated Society of Tailors being supplied with 'a handsome silk banner – upon one side was the arms of the Tailors Company and upon the back were medallions showing the various objects of the Society'. Although this confirms the tailors' union made use of the armorial bearings of the Worshipful Company of Merchant Tailors (one of the twelve great companies) granted arms in 1586, the blazon does not appear to have been favoured by the tailors for wide use. Far more popular was a design which derived inspiration from the Worshipful Company of Needlemakers which depicted the figures of Adam and Eve, wreathed about the waist with fig leaves – the first suit of clothes. As early as 1832 a contemporary account of the Edinburgh Reform Celebration records that among those taking part was the St Andrew's Society of Tailors, whose flag 'of green silk, a royal tent in chief and lion passant gardent in gold crest, a tree and serpent, supporters Adam and Eve as large as life; motto – *Nudus et amici vitis me*'. They also carried a second banner of blue silk with a shield in the centre, bearing a pair of gilded shears. The motto above read 'Knowledge is power', and below, two hands joined and underneath, 'A man's a man for a' that'. The Phoenix Society of Tailors carried a 'very splendid new flag'; design – in the centre a gilt shield resting upon a phoenix, the shield surmounted by thistles and surmounted with a helmet over which is a tree with a serpent and the inscription 'The Phoenix Society of Tailors'; supporters of the shield – Adam and Eve; motto – '*Nudus et amici vitis me*'.

The Permanent Amalgamated Farriers' Protection Society, founded in 1808, used the arms of the Worshipful Company of Farriers, incorporated on 17 June 1673, on their banner until the start of the twentieth century. They added two mottoes, 'Labour is the source of all wealth' and 'United to support but not combined to injure'. The 1896 banners of the National Association of Operative Plasterers, formed in 1872, and the Metropolitan Society of Operative Plasterers both bear the arms of the Worshipful Company of Plasterers who were incorporated by charter in 1500. The Metropolitan Society strengthened the guild motto 'Let brotherly love continue' with the addition of the words 'Labour conquers everything' and the illustration of a cap of liberty. There is an account in the *Pioneer* of 7 December 1833 of a procession of trade unionists of Birmingham to the ceremony for laying the foundation stone of the builders' guildhall. The procession included 'plasterers, wearing aprons with bibs and preceded by the arms of the trade etched in gold and framed, decorated with laurel and surmounted with a crown of laurel and two coloured rosettes'. The motto on the banner read 'Let brotherly love continue'. A second banner of the plasterers bore the slogan 'May the trowel and brush never fail' and 'Success to the United Plasterers'. Boilermakers and Brushmakers, Paviors, Coopers, Painters and Coachmakers, all adopted and adapted guild arms and dates of incorporation to give respectability and establishment. When craft-skilled trade unionists emigrated, they took the tradition with them as evidenced by the banner of the Sheet Metal Working Industrial Union of Australia, which carries the guild arms and the words 'Incorporated by King Charles II December 29th. 1670'! The South African Operative Masons' Society, founded in 1896, inscribed their banner with a list of the world's great architecture, laying claim to the building of the Parthenon, the Colosseum and Notre Dame.

Practically all the craft unions made at least some use of the traditional mottoes, emblems and symbols of the guilds, borrowing in part, if not in entirety. They sought to trace the origins of their craft, if not their organisation, in order to justify their claims to represent the best interests of the trade and not only the welfare of the men. The Operative Society of Bricklayers, London Order, founded on 8 April 1848, and the Manchester Order used the same illustrations on their banners, which were probably used earlier on the banners of the Friendly Society of Operative Bricklayers, founded in 1829. These showed the first bricklayers building the Tower of Babel and the completed cities of Rome and London. This design was very popular and contined to be used well into the twentieth century. It is also to be found on the banner of the Amalgamated Union of Building Trade Workers, Norwich branch, formed only in 1921.

In their efforts to acquire a ready-made history and strengthen their position in the eyes of the community, the bricklayers were not alone in looking backwards to the biblical forebears of their crafts, as if to imply a direct descendancy, an unbroken link from earliest times. While the bricklayers quoted Genesis, the shipwrights looked to Noah and the tinsmiths to Tubal Cain as the first worker in metals. The tailors, as we have said, claimed the making of the first suit of clothes for Adam and Eve, leaving the printers to appear as newcomers, tracing their origins to Gutenberg, Caxton and Alois Senefelder. It was left to the Carpenters to make the most audacious claim of all, depicting Joseph of Nazareth and declaring him 'the most distinguished member of our craft on record'. Whilst biblical antecedents and spurious coats of arms were contrived to bring immediate respectability, there is one instance of a savage parody of armorial bearings inscribed on a banner of 1833, during the agitation for the Ten-Hours Bill. The factory system had become dominant in the rapidly growing towns in Yorkshire and Lancashire and children in the cotton and woollen industries supplied the bulk of the labour force. Even in well-run mills there were children from seven years of age working from six in the morning until seven at night, six days a week, with the strap of the overseer to keep

them awake. A massive movement, led by Richard Oastler, developed to force candidates at a coming election to support a bill to introduce a ten-hour working day. At a mass meeting at Wisbey a crowd of 100,000 people with banners and bands assembled; a graphic description of the banners is recorded by Alfred in his *History of the Factory Movement*. Many of the banners were made specifically for the meeting and cannot be classified as permanent trade union banners. Some, however, which seem to have been professional work 'of costly materials and the device skilfully executed', must have been intended for a longer period of use. One is a classic of its kind. 'The arms on the banner comprised a large shield on which was painted a billey-roller, a timeclock, a screw key and a knotted strap, the whole supported by a couple of cripples'. The timeclock would have shown the hands at five in the morning, when the children had to rise for work or even to be at work in many of the worst factories; the knotted strap was the overseer's implement for enforcing discipline and wakefulness. The crippled supporters were a biting comment on the future of factory children by the time they had grown to maturity. Other banners described by W.R. Croft in *Oastler and His Times* include one depicting a scene of 'the good Samaritan staunching the wounds of a poor man', a scene to be popular with trade unionists for embellishing their banners over the next hundred years. Another showed a factory overlooker, strapping a child into a factory at ten minutes past five in the morning. This banner was described as 'of fair artistic merit'.

The full horror of factory life of the period seems to have been covered by the trade union banners during the period of the agitation. A moving account is given of a banner painting showing

> a father carrying his little girl through a pelting storm of sleet and snow to a noted flax mill near Leeds, at five in the morning, himself in tatters and having taken off his own remnants of what was once his coat, to carry his hapless baby who was doomed to earn her parents' living as well as her own, at the certain destruction of her own health and morals and probably her very life, doomed to a premature grave.

Others had inscribed 'Father, is it time?', a cry which was often heard the night through in the crowded and wretched dormitories of the factory working people, and which little children, more asleep than awake (dreading the consequences of being late) were often heard to utter.

The trade unions without craft traditions looked to friendly societies, Masonic lodges and churches for the inspiration for the designs and mottoes for their banners. They and the craft unions also copied the rituals and the regalia of such organisations, including oaths, initiation ceremonies, the regalia of office and structure of the organisations.

The earliest detailed account of the making of a trade union banner, that of the United Society of Weavers, describes the symbols that made up the total illustration, which included the 'all-seeing eye of the Omnipotent King of Kings, looking down and diffusing the rays of glory on all beneath that never fail to light the path of the earnest worker and fearless spirit who believes in His love and almighty power'. This ancient symbol, so widely used by Masons and friendly societies, is featured in hundreds of trade union banners up to the period of the First World War. Perhaps the fearless spirits who went off to Flanders thought the path a little dim after that experience, for as a trade union device it does not seem to have appeared on any banners made after 1918.

The manufacture of the banner of the United Weavers is recounted by F. Warner, the famous founder of the firm of silkweavers of that name, in his book on the silk industry. It is an astonishing story of what must be the most expensive banner ever made for a trade union. The Benevolent Society of Weavers was founded in 1802. The organisers were men of sound business judgement who decided to invest the funds in bank stock. Unfortunately, the treasurer misappropriated the funds, and this so disheartened the majority of the members that they withdrew from the union. After some deliberation, the few remaining members decided to share what was left of the money and broke up the society. But during its short existence the union embarked on what was in effect a publicity promotion to combat the declining state of the English silk industry. Frank Warner wrote that 'in the first quarter of the nineteenth century, the plight of the Spitalfields silk weavers seems to have been at its worst and the degradation of the district at its lowest point'. The plan was to produce a banner that would be 'an example of silk weaving of such superlative exellence as to confound those persons especially amongst the nobility and gentry of this country, who imagined that English silk weaving was inferior to that of the French'. The union hoped the public exhibition of such an example of their work would put an end to this false belief and boost the home trade. The idea seems to have survived the premature demise of the United Weavers, and a committee of five of the original founders met at a public house, The Knave of Clubs, and decided to continue with the scheme. They formed a national flag committee of eleven men, including delegates from a number of their connected societies. On 18 June 1807 they issued an appeal for money which was successful enough to start the work. The banner was to be two yards (1.80 m) wide, of a rich crimson satin and brocaded on both sides alike.

A designer named G. Blatch received three guineas for making an elaborate drawing. The design rehearsed many of the characteristic features of nineteenth-century banners. Under the all-seeing eye, 'a female figure of pensive aspect' laments over a remnant of brocade. Enterprise, assisted by Genius, kneels to revive her, a cornucopia pours out plenty, the weavers' arms are planted on the temple of fame and while the corners sport emblems of Peace, Industry and Commerce, a beautiful border rehearses the same themes. The design being approved, a workshop was taken, preparations for weaving were made and a draughtsman and operative weaver were chosen. The actual weaving was started at the beginning of 1808, and by October of that year subscribers were invited to see work in progress.

The committee approached the Society of Arts asking for inspection of the work and encouragement of the weavers. The society was duly impressed and struck a silver medal which was presented by the president of the society, the Duke of Norfolk, on 30 May 1809. Alert as ever to the publicity to be gained from such recognition, the flag committee printed 1,000 bills appealing for subscriptions. Unfortunately, little was raised and debts were accumulating. In 1810 advertisements were inserted in *The Times*, the *Morning Chronicle* and the *Morning Post*, inviting the fashionable world to view and support the banner. To this invitation only one person responded, a Mr Kinkaid, and the treasurer suggested he should attempt to interest the Queen and Princesses in the work. A copper plate of the flag was engraved and a frame impression together with a letter from the committee to the Queen, entrusted to that gentleman to convey to Her Majesty and their Royal Highnesses, who were then at Windsor. The Queen replied that she much appreciated the present of the engraving and gladly allowed it to be dedicated to her, but she could not arrange to visit London to see the work. Thus, grudgingly supported by the trade, ignored by the members of fashionable society whom they had hoped to astonish, and disappointed of royal patronage, the committee bravely persevered until 23 March 1811, at which date the work was completed. It had taken two men, T. Frank and T. Atkins, Junior, three years to draft and weave. The total contributions amounted to £571. 17s. 4d. and the committee found themselves in debt to the sum of £381. 4s. 0d., not counting their own expenses. The weavers' banner, after having thus cost nearly £1,000, was first sent to the Society of Arts who, having inspected it, voted a bounty of ten guineas towards the expenses. It was next exhibited at a public house in Bethnal Green where few besides the poor weavers themselves saw it. After a short time, it was so neglected that it disappeared. It was generally supposed to have been stolen by some emissary of the weavers' hated rivals, the French. The union of representative silkweavers, burdened with debt, seems to have survived this crushing disappointment but a little later the flag committee, if one may judge from the remarks of the author of the quaint pamphlet in which this story has been preserved, bitterly regretted the unfortunate undertaking.

In 1834, in connection with their joining the Grand

National Consolidated Trades Union, we have an account of the Nantwich shoemakers having a trade banner made, 'emblematical of the trade' painted by a 'Herald painter', Thomas W. Jones of Hospital Street at a cost of £25, an enormous sum of money equal to a year's wages for a labourer. It carried an illustration of St Crispin and the motto 'May the manufactures of the sons of St Crispin be trod upon by all the world'. Years later there was an amusing sequel when in 1893, at a Trades Union Congress parade in Belfast, the Orangemen mistook the bearded St Crispin on the banner of the National Union of Boot and Shoe Operatives for 'their Arch Antipathy' and at cries of 'to hell with the Pope' the banner bearers had to flee, to escape the Protestant wrath. Both the slogan and the patron saint were featured on banners of the National Union of Boot and Shoe Operatives well into the twentieth century, a fine example being that of the Nos. 1 and 2 branches, Northampton, made in the late 1920s and in regular use until 1962.

From the 1840s the form and appearance of the banners was to remain basically the same, although the illustrations and slogans would alter over the years to meet the changes in society and trade unionism. Following the repeal of the Combination Acts, they were no longer modest-sized flags to be displayed in meeting rooms, but grew to huge dimensions. A cordwainers' banner of the 1860s was described as 'as big as the mainsail of a good sized barque'. Havelock Wilson, the founder of the National Amalgamated Seamen's and Firemen's Union, told of a banner made in 1850 that may have been the largest trade union banner of all time.

> It would have made an excellent drop scene for a music hall or theatre. It was not painted on silk, but on ship's canvas, as used for making sails. The members had requested that it should be extra large, and as the ordinary weavers' looms were not big enough to make it, they had a special loom constructed for the purpose. The seamen of Dover's day (George Dover was secretary of a Sunderland seamen's union in 1850) were intensely patriotic as well as being strong Nationalists and Imperialists. Therefore, it was not surprising to find on one side of the banner a picture of Queen Victoria with sceptre and crown, sandwiched between two huge lions. Behind the Queen in a semi-circle stood half-a-dozen sailors. They were life size, dressed in the garb of the day, with short blue jackets, white trousers and glossy straw hats. One or two of the men carried telescopes, for, I presume, the purpose of attempting to look into the future. On the reverse side of the banner was a representation of half-a-dozen ships wrecked on a lee shore, several drowned seamen lying about, with widows and children kneeling beside them. The banner was so heavy and so large that the men only attempted to carry it on one occasion, and that was when a strong breeze was blowing. The result was that the banner and its bearers landed 'all in a heap'. After this episode, whenever any important occasion arose the banner was suspended from one friendly public house to another by stout ropes. Such houses for the time being were designated as 'headquarters', and it is scarcely necessary to say that they did a 'roaring trade'.

No banner was complete without a motto. Usually this was a biblical quotation, a translation from the Latin of an appropriate guild motto, a line or two of doggerel from the branch secretary, or more frequently classic lines, often taken out of context if they fitted the union message. Early nineteenth-century mottoes were essentially defensive and conciliatory in content. The emphasis was on brotherly help for one another, simple pleas for a decent life and reassurances that no harm was intended to the trade. The most popular motto seems to have been variations on the theme of 'Combined to protect, but not to injure'. Others included 'Reason not force', 'The labourer is worthy of his hire' (Luke 10:7), 'Let us live by our labours' and frequently expressed hopes that 'the trade may flourish'. There were exceptions; even in the 1830s some inscriptions already hinted at defiance and the need for social change. 'Union is strength', 'Knowledge is power' (Proverbs 24:5, 'A man of knowledge increaseth in strength'), and 'Just laws and equal rights' are among the more progressive mottoes to be found at that time. In September 1833 the Builders' Union held its Annual Conference (the Builders' Parliament) in Manchester and heard Robert Owen disclose his 'great secret' that 'labour is the source of all wealth'. This was to be emblazoned as a favourite motto on hundreds of union banners right up to the First World War.

In 1831 it was recorded that 'a large meeting of miners was held at Jarrow, each colliery beating a banner with the name of the colliery and various mottoes'. This was during the great strike of that year, a time when miners were virtually slaves, bound by the 'yearly bond'. The miners' emancipation from the bond in 1872 is commemorated on some banners even to this day. In the following year, 1832, there was a political procession of the miners of Durham and Northumberland, described by Richard Fynes as 'bearing numerous banners, of the gayest description, nearly all being embellished with a painted design and with a motto, more or less connected with the recent struggle between the miners and their employers' (the great strike of 1832). The mottoes on the banners are unfortunately not recorded, but as the strike involved the coal-owning Marquis of Londonderry calling out cavalry, foot yeomanry and two troops of the Third Dragoons against the strikers, it is unlikely that the 'mottoes' were of a conciliatory nature. More likely they would have best been described as slogans.

In 1844 the oppressed miners of Northumberland and Durham again struck work and there is a precise report of 'seventy-two banners . . . bearing appropriate mottoes'. 'Nothing could be more imposing than the sight of the men marching in procession as they came to the Town Moor'. It required courage indeed to march with the union banner in those days when the coalowners evicted whole villages in their efforts to break the union. Fynes tells of

> Pregnant women, bedridden men, children in the cradle, remorselessly turned out . . . the breaking of their furniture to pieces and the throwing of their household goods, with their food, into the road . . . aged, sick and feeble women forced from the homes of their childhood . . . the cruel eviction of men who had met with accidents in the pit before the strike commenced.

When starving and homeless, the workhouses were closed to them and the Marquis issued a notice forbidding the local tradesmen to give credit or supplies to the miners or their families. It is related that the miners

> bore every outrage and indignity without physical remonstrance . . . It was not because they were cowards, but they were taught it was the object of the coal-owners to make them break the peace, so that they could fill the prisons, transport and hang them as they had done in 1832 and thus break up the union and enslave the generations to follow.

In the end, the strike was broken and the banners were hidden away in the rafters of the miners' cottages.

Elsewhere, trade union banners were openly paraded in support of strikers, the Reform Movement, the Chartists, the National League for the Independence of Poland and for every progressive cause that stood for the greater liberty of working people. On 21 April 1834, at a mighty demonstration at Copenhagen Fields, London, to protest at the transportation of the six agricultural workers from Tolpuddle, the unions, organised by the Grand National Consolidated Trades Union, assembled at seven in the morning, 'with banners of the different lodges flying in the breeze'. By eight o'clock, it is reported, the roads were filled with a mass of men and the banners were supported by a well disciplined corps. a contemporary print shows the workers led by thirty-three banners, each man decorated by a red ribbon.

When Garibaldi visited London in 1864 the trade unions with their banners marched to honour him. In 1866, in the famous battle of Hyde Park when the railings were torn down, the gates being closed to the Reform demonstrators, it was trade union banners which led the way. In the same year, in the Reform demonstrations at Brook Fields, Birmingham, hundreds of thousands of people representing reform societies, benefit clubs and trade unions 'marched to the meeting ground with banners flying and bands playing in a column near upon two miles in length'. The procession included ironworkers and miners of south Staffordshire, nailmakers and carpetweavers of east Worcestershire and the ribbon and woollen and cottonmakers of north Warwickshire. Engineers and carriage builders, gunmakers and jewellers, carpenters and painters, the shoemakers of Birmingham, the japanners of Wolverhampton, the glasscutters of Stourbridge, the lockmakers of Willenhall, the glassblowers of Oldsbury, the alkali workers of Smethwick, the paper workers and agricultural workers of Kings Norton, all with their banners.

As the unions grew in strength and the amalgamation of local societies began to establish national organisations like the Amalgamated Society of Engineers (1851) and the Amalgamated Society of Carpenters and Joiners (1860) the branches sought to mark their identity by having their own banners made in addition to the banner of the national organisation. The national organisations with central control of funds left it to the branches to make their own arrangements for banners and to raise the money as best they could. With so many small craft unions centred on single towns or even single factories, and with the branches of the large unions being responsible for their own banners, a grass-roots picture of the aims, hopes and fears of these nineteenth-century trade unionists emerged in picture form on their banners. The banners became a familiar part of industrial and political life.

Trade unionists turned quite naturally to the tools of the trade, place of work and the products of their labours as symbols of identity. Such banners had not only the advantage of ready recognition, but association of the union with its craft. They were also an honest reflection of the pride of the workers for their craft skills and their genuine concern for the quality and prosperity of the trade. There were already early examples; in 1832 the Associated Carpenters of Scotland illustrated their banner with the city coat of arms, adding two supporters, one carrying a handsaw, the other a jack plane. These two figures, symbols of the trade, were to be incorporated in the beautiful emblem designed by A.J. Waudby for the Society of Carpenters and Joiners in 1866 and have been used by woodworkers on banner designs until the 1960s. The Edinburgh carpenters in 1860 included a large sideboard in the design of their banner, while the Leith Shipwrights showed an illustration of a four-masted man-of-war on the stocks. The craft unions were not merely proud, but jealous of their skills and the 'mysteries of the craft' and did not extend the hand of brotherhood to unskilled workers, as the motto on a banner of the Operative Stonemasons testifies: 'Let us support our trade and keep out others that would invade.' Slowly, the imagery of trade unionism was to be shaped by work and struggle, printers, bakers, coopers, painters, shoemakers and countless other crafts followed the style. Towards the end of the century, the practice had gone far beyond the traditional trades and included workers, who if they could not easily depict their skills or products of their work, could and did illustrate where they worked. Two good examples are a banner of the Flax Dressers Trade and Benevolent Trade Union who showed the interior of a vast flax dressing and sorting factory on their banner and the National Municipal and Incorporated Vestry Employees' Labour Union who depicted their members mending the cobbled road in front of a Vestry Hall.

The use of banners in trade union struggles continued to grow. In 1863 the Durham miners were fighting the enslaving contract system known as the 'yearly bond' and there is an account of how 'old banners that had been folded away in the houses of some men since the memorable strike of 1844, were brought out again and unfurled'. The first Trades Union Congress was held in 1868, with forty unions representing 118,367 members and trade unionism grew rapidly, spreading beyond the skilled artisans to include the wider sectors of industry. The agricultural workers were organised by Joseph Arch in 1872 and in the same year the Amalgamated Society of Railway Servants was formed. The previous year the miners of Durham held their first 'big meeting', at Wharton Park, under the auspices of the Durham Miners' Mutual Confident Association annual Galas. The men walked from the colliery villages to Durham City, carts and wagons bringing their wives and sweethearts. Alexander McDonald addressed the men before the banner of the Thornley lodge, which bore the motto 'A fair day's pay for a fair day's work'. He told of boys working fifteen and sixteen hours a day, Brancepeth colliery being cited as an example. A poetic miners' leader from Staffordshire recited and sang during his speech, leading the company 'most heartily in singing

All men are equal in his sight,
The bond, the free, the black, the white,
He made them all, them freedom gave,
He made the man, man made the slave.'

The *Durham County Advertiser*, reporting the big meeting, wrote, 'upwards of seventy silk banners especially designed and emblazoned were present on the occasion . . . extremely handsome in design' and attributing them to a London firm (obviously, George Tutill's), the cost being 'computed at £2,500'. The report also concludes that there were some amateur productions by collier artists that were 'by no means discreditable'.

Everywhere, trade unionism was on the march. the economic boom of 1871-2 had brought a marked expansion of small societies and the increasing consolidation of the pioneer craft unions. By 1874 over 150 unions had affiliated to the TUC, representing 1,191,922 members. But at this time there was a period of recurrent economic crises which encouraged fierce and determined attacks by the employers. The small societies, their funds decimated by unemployment benefits, wilted before the onslaught, no fewer than 320 unions being founded and dissolved between 1872 and 1875. The old craft unions remained firm, but many, like the masons, ironfounders and carpenters, had become so heavily orientated towards the benevolent and friendly aspects of trade unionism that they were hardly more than 'sick and burial clubs', afraid of the financial consequences of supporting strikes, even against wage cuts or increased hours. Wage cuts were forced onto Lancashire cotton workers and South Wales miners, and longer hours on Scottish engineers. But new and influential craftsmen trade unionists were appearing, highly critical of the old union policies; men like Tom Mann, John Burns and Fred Hammill, who were turning to socialism to solve the perpetual crises of capitalism. Basing their unionism on the concept of class solidarity they looked beyond the confines of craft unionism to the mass of unskilled and unorganised workers, and campaigned for a new trade unionism that would embrace the semi-skilled and the labourers. A new spirit developed which was to culminate in the events of 1888-9, the Bryant and May's match girls' strike, the organisation of the London gas workers by Will Thorne and the revolt of the London dockers led by Ben Tillett, bringing in a new vigour and militancy to the building of trade unionism. 1889 was to be the year of the 'new unionism' and of the manufacture of the greatest number of trade union banners ever made in one year.

THE HOPE OF LABOUR

'All along the Commercial Road the women turned out in thousands to see their husbands and their sons pass in triumph. The sun seemed brighter, the music more inspiriting, the banners more in number than ever before.' The procession was that led by Ben Tillett and John Burns, marching in triumph at the head of the victorious dockers on their way to Hyde Park on 15 September 1889 to celebrate the successful outcome of their historic fight for union recognition and the 6d. per hour rate. The background to this great strike, one of the most momentous in trade union history, is nowhere better described than in Ben Tillett's own pamphlet, 'A dock labourer's bitter cry', written in 1887. Tillett described the dockers as 'Lazaruses who starve upon the crumbs from the rich man's table' and told of how the men, to obtain casual employment, were driven daily into a shed, iron-barred from end to end, while the contractor walked up and down with the air of a dealer in a cattle market, picking and choosing the strongest men, who fought each other like beasts for the chance of a ticket which would mean, at the most, four hours' work for less than 6d. an hour. It was to combat this brutal existence that Tillett led the men of the Cutler Street Warehouse in July 1887 to form the Tea Operatives' and General Labourers' Association. One of the first decisions taken by the union was to have a banner made; not a large one, for there were no funds to indulge in the extravagance of a grand banner after the style of the skilled and organised stevedores. It was a simple affair, described by Tillett as 'a linen sheet on which was thickly painted in black, the name of our organisation'. The slogan on the banner urged all dock workers and general labourers to join the union and 'defend the rights of manhood in a practical and direct manner'. A noble appeal, but no easy task, as dockside meetings with the banner meant 'mud and road refuse as a bouquet only too often'.

In other parts of London, unskilled and previously unorganised labour was also on the move. In July 1888 the successful socialist-led strike of the Bryant and May match girls secured wide publicity and exposed the shocking conditions under which they worked. Engels referred to the strike as the 'light jostle needed for the entire avalanche to follow'. At Beckton Gasworks, the following year, Will Thorne led the men who worked a twelve hour shift and a thirteen day fortnight in a successful struggle for an eight hour day and a twelve day fortnight. At a meeting in Victoria Park on 20 May 1889, addressed by Will Thorne, two thousand gas workers launched the Amalgamated Society of Gasworkers and formally adopted the motto 'Love, unity, fidelity', which was to grace their banners and the banners of the National Union of General and Municipal Workers for the next fifty years.

Eventually on 13 August 1889, a small group of labourers struck work at the South West India Docks. Included in the demands presented by Tillett was the claim for wages to be raised to 6d. per hour. The Great Dock Strike had started. A colourful and important part of the dockers' struggle was the daily marches through the streets of the capital. The lively processions with bands and banners served to strengthen the comradeship and unity of the hungry strikers, raise money and awake the public. The sight of Tillett and Burns at the head of 10,000 ragged men aroused both pity and fear. The first march saw some forty-one banners, though 'some were no more than red rags on poles'. Each day the procession was repeated, the number of banners growing as trade unions and friendly societies lent support. When on 19 August the stevedores joined the strike, their magnificent banner fluttered at the head of 10,000 men, the union banners supplemented by the banners of friendly societies, including the Foresters and the Sons of the Phoenix. In the march were Doggett's prize winners, a 'stalwart battalion of watermen marching proudly in long scarlet coats, pink stockings and velvet caps'. The strike cost nearly £43,000 and included payment of £1,251. 18s. 2½d. to 'pickets and banner bearers' and £936. 1s. 6d. for hire of bands. Money to support the strike had come from many quarters, some unexpected, including the Salvation Army. The greatest contribution, however, came from the colonies, with more than £25,000 coming from Australia alone. After the strike, as the Dock, Wharf, Riverside and General Labourers' Union grew rapidly (adding 200,000 members in one year) branch after branch acknowledged the generous support of the Australian workers by having the unity of British and Australian dockers portrayed hand in hand on their banners. The stevedores too used the same design and it seems to have been repeated for some thirty years. The banner of the old Barking branch of the Dock, Wharf, Riverside and General Labourers' Union carries the device, along with a portrait of a young Ernie Bevin. The banners of the dockers were made in huge numbers in the years following the strike. Corn porters, coalies, ballast heavers, crane drivers, deal porters, fruit porters, all joined in the enthusiastic upsurge of trade unionism by proclaiming their purpose on silk. The mottoes, slogans and illustrations were as varied as the individual groups who formed themselves into the new unions and new branches of the Dockers' Union. One militant section, the export branch of the Dockers' Union, depicted on their banner a heroic docker wrestling with the serpent of capitalism. The slogans included 'This is a holy war and we shall not cease until all destitution, prostitution and exploitation is swept away.' This was in accord with the thinking of the leadership headed by Tom Mann and Ben Tillett,

DOCK, WHARF, RIVERSIDE AND GENERAL LABOURERS' UNION

Of Great Britain and Ireland.

President: TOM MANN.   Treasurer: F. N. CHARRINGTON, L.C.C.   Gen. Sec.: BEN TILLETT.

Registered Office: 33, MILE END ROAD, E.

Our Motto: "A Nation Made free by love, a mighty Brotherhood Linked by a jealous interchange of good."

VICTORIA & ALBERT DOCK DISTRICT.

A MASS MEETING

WILL TAKE PLACE ON

Sunday, July 5th, 1891,

AT

MORLEY'S CORNER, BARKING ROAD,

AT 4 P.M.

When Addresses will be delivered by the following Friends of Labour, on the Benefits of Trades Unionism and Labour Representation:

PLATFORM No. 1.	PLATFORM No. 2.
CHAIRMAN:	CHAIRMAN:
BRO. TOM WATTS, D.L.U.	**COUNCILLOR GEO. LAMBERT**
	Labour Candidate North West Ham. D. L. U.
SPEAKERS:	SPEAKERS
BEN TILLLETT, JOHN BURNS,	TOM MANN, J. H. WILSON,
D.L.U. L.C.C.	D.L.U. Gen. Sec. Seamen and Firemen's Union.
TOM McCARTHY,	W. THORNE, DR. JOHN MOIR.
D.L.U.	Gen. Sec. Gas Workers' Union.
KEIR HARDIE, MR. RATCLIFF,	
Labour Candidate South West Ham. Solicitor D. L. U.	

ON WHICH OCCASION THE

HANDSOME NEW SILK BANNER

Of the TIDAL BASIN No. 3 BRANCH will be unfurled by

JOHN BURNS and KEIR HARDIE.

A Grand Procession will start from the District Office, 225, Victoria Dock Road, at 2.30 p.m., and march through the principal Streets to Morley's Corner.

All Trade Unions are cordially invited.

COME IN YOUR THOUSANDS AND SUPPORT TRADE UNIONISM.

ALL SHOULD READ THE "TRADE UNIONIST."

W. KRANC, Branch Secretary.   H. STYLES, District Secretary.
TOM WATTS, Branch Chairman.   J. FAIRBAIRN, District Chairman.

GEO. REYNOLDS, 23, Stepney Green, London, E.

who saw the union not as a benefit society but as an instrument for social change. At the same time, not all the scattered branches grasped the significance of the union challenge to the employers. The Ipswich branch emblazoned their banner with a docker shaking hands with an employer, with the slogan, 'May they ever be united'. The Ballast Heavers' Protection Society continued to use the old craft motto 'Defence not defiance', while the United Stevedores' Protection League settled for 'Union and victory'. For illustrations to enliven the banners, the combined imaginations of the dockers and the banner painters knew no bounds. While one group depicted its members as Roman centurions, another embellished their banner with the figure of King John. The majority, however, settled for scenes which showed the daily activities of the men, fruit porters unloading oranges, apples, nuts and grapes from a steamship, coalwhippers at work on a steam collier, dockers with sack hooks, in fact every facet of work in which the men engaged at the busy wharves and docks of the Thames. As the unions grew, so the banners proliferated. Almost the first step upon setting up a new branch was to order a banner. Each branch announced its birth with an impressive public unfurling ceremony at which union leaders, civic dignitaries and fraternal delegates would participate. When the tugboat branch of the National Amalgamated Seamen's and Firemen's Union unfurled their new colour on 1 November 1890, they booked the Queen's Music Hall, Poplar, for the event. Presided over by Tom Mann and Tom McCarthy, the founder of the branch, a delegate from the Australian strikers, a Mr Fitzgerald, unveiled the banner to the delight of the packed audience and the accompaniment of the Seamen's Union band dressed in maritime attire. The banner was described as 'a splendid addition to the colours of trade unionism'.

A few days later, it was the turn of the 'coalies' to unfurl their banner at Whitechapel to mark the foundation of the Kentish Town branch. 'With bands, banners and bannerettes, the ceremony was held in the open air with Chinese lanterns and oriental "dips"'. Even the rain did not dampen the high spirits of the 'boisterous boys who spent a jolly evening'. In the same month the Bermondsey No.3 branch of the Watermen and Lightermen of the River Thames packed Bermondsey Town Hall to watch the unveiling of 'a real work of art by George Tutill', the banners of the Stepney, Greenwich, Blackwall, Wapping and Northfleet branches decorating the stage for the event. When the proceedings had terminated, they formed up outside the Town Hall with bands playing and banners flying and marched to the Southwark Tavern, where 'another meeting of festive character was held'. Throughout the docks and ports of Britain, scarcely a week passed without similar ceremonies during the years following the Great Dock Strike.

The demand for banners was not confined to the waterside unions, but spread through every organised trade in Britain. Large sums of money were spent on banners which grew in size and lavishness as unions vied with one another to claim the most magnificent banner. They were not only carried in support of strikes or demonstrations but turned out in support of hospital days, churches, guild processions, funerals and town carnivals. An account of a hospital day parade in Sussex in 1890 tells of the unions, which included housepainters, bakers, engineers, railway workers, ironfounders, carpenters and builders, formed up with their 'banners either new, or kept jealously out of sight'. When the United Society of French Polishers went on their annual outing to Hampstead Heath on 24 May 1896, they proudly took their banner with them.

In their effort to portray their trades, their purpose, their hopes and fears, the branches developed banner illustrations into an elaborate and telling popular art. One of the favourite forms of illustration during the 1890s was the picture parable, which showed with Sunday school simplicity the bad and good effects of two different courses of action. The concept was not new and was widely used in Victorian times by every sort of 'do good' organisation. The employers used pictures to show that bad timekeeping led to the sack, while punctuality brought prosperity. The Temperance Movement showed that drink led to misery and broken homes while abstinence was rewarded with health and happiness. The trade unions readily utilised pictures extensively on their banners in support of the Eight-Hours Movement, graphically illustrating the difference in the quality of life between twelve or sixteen hours' work and eight hours' work. This form of picture parable was used to great effect by the Wigan miners, where one half of their banner illustrated a miner returned home after twelve hours' work. He was shown as too exhausted to care for his food and his child was in her nightdress, ready for bed. The other half depicted a miner returned home after eight hours' work. He was seen sitting comfortably to his tea, his evening paper by him and happily holding his wide-awake child.

The Amalgamated Society of Railway Servants used the theme of safety in a similar way to demand shorter hours. Under the caption 'thirteen hours', a signalman was seated in his box exhausted from overwork and oblivious to the fact that the signal was down and the points open, although a train which should have been stopped was already in sight. Opposite, the signalman was seen leaving work after eight hours, his wife and child coming to meet him, while his post is taken by another man, full of energy through having enough time for rest and recreation. The reverse side of this splendid banner, painted in 1896, depicted the bustle and departure of a train from King's Cross Station and bore a strong resemblance to W.P. Frith's well-known painting *The*

Railway Station. The amount of detailed work involved in the painting of this large banner must put it among the most ambitious of the trade union banners ever produced by Tutill's.

The fight against child labour in the mines was also featured on miners' banners in the same style. The illustration was of two little boys, one in the pink of condition, the other pale and emaciated. 'I go to school,' says the first. 'I go to the mine,' says the second. Some of the scenes were not without humour. In 1872 the Sunnybrow banner of the Durham miners showed a pit pony energetically declaring for the Eight-Hours Movement and refusing to draw his load until he obtained the same terms as his companion in other districts.

A whole series of parable pictures were produced by Tutill's entitled 'Two sides of the question', and were extremely popular from 1918 until 1939. These showed the difference between the organised worker, well fed and well dressed, and the unorganised worker, ill fed and poorly clad. The Victorian obsession with moralising on self-help still lingered on in these banner pictures, the moral being quite clear: self-help meant joining your trade union. Towards the latter part of the last century the tradition developed of honouring public figures by painting their portraits on union banners. The origins of the tradition are obscure though it developed at a time when erecting statues and public presentations to Empire builders and Victorian statesmen were much in vogue. The first portraits to be used were those of politicians rather than trade union leaders. They were Liberal and even Conservative MPs who had some connection with the trade or district on which the union was based and who were known to have spoken in favour of the trade or defended the wider interests of the men in Parliament or local government. Very few portrait banners made before 1900 survive, probably because memories are short. The civic leaders honoured during the 1880s and 1890s were nearly all forgotten by 1918 and the banners would have been discarded or overpainted by a new generation of trade unionists engaged in their own fierce struggle against the employers during the 1920s.

The 1895 banner of the Boilermakers' and Iron and Steel Shipbuilders' Society, Barrow No.3 branch, depicted the general secretary of the union, but he had to share place of honour with a portrait of the Duke of Devonshire, who presided over a Royal Commission on Labour in 1891. Earlier, the West Pelton colliers had emblazoned their banner with a fine portrait of Alexander McDonald, the Liberal MP and miners' spokesman, but he too had to share the glory, this time with W.E. Gladstone. The South Pelaw lodge of the Durham Miners' Association featured Messrs Crawford and Storey, both MPs, and a London dockside union chose Cunninghame Graham, MP. The National Union of Clickers and Rough Staff Cutters had likenesses of their president

and general secretary painted on their banner in 1895, and the 'coalies' their secretary, James O'Connor, in 1890. Haswell lodge of the Durham Miners' Association portrayed three pioneers of mining trade unionism, Tommy Ramsey, Alexander McDonald and William Crawford, early in the 1890s with the inscription, 'They being dead yet speaketh'. It was not until the rise of the 'new unionism' that the practice of portraying national trade union leaders became widespread, Tillett, Burns, Mann and Thorne being eulogised in this way. Many branches, lodges and small societies would have honoured their officials and other public figures with such portraits, encouraged by the banner painter who advertised 'public men, members of Parliament and Presidents of Lodges and Branches can be painted on silk banners at a small extra charge'.

The names of working class leaders who have been portrayed on the banners is a roll of fame in labour history. Keir Hardie, Robert Smillie, George Lansbury, Ramsay MacDonald, A.J. Cook, Joseph Arch, Nye Bevan, Manny Shinwell, Arthur Horner, James Larkin, Clement Attlee and, of course, Marx and Lenin, have all been acclaimed. The tradition continues to this day, with such diverse figures as Hugh Gaitskell and Arthur Scargill to be found adorning banners. But the idolatry of man is an uncertain affair. The anger of the rank and file at the 'treachery' of Ramsay MacDonald and Philip Snowden in 1930 is reflected by the scarcity of banners bearing their portraits which survive the period, despite the fact that both men had often been celebrated in the years beforehand. Ronald Caffyn, a former manager of Tutill's, explained how the banners bearing their portraits flooded back from the lodges to his studio. Just as the brush of the artist could give the stroke of immortality, so could it paint it out with equal ease. The miserable pair were painted off the banners and replaced with local agents, loyal MPs and militants like Cook. The fury of the men is best conveyed by Caffyn who relates

> The banners were not just returned, they were mutilated. I remember one banner from Durham which had MacDonald's eyes cut out. We had to patch the banner before we could overpaint it with the face of a local man. Another was returned with 'traitor to labour' daubed across MacDonald's face.

Sometimes, in an ever-changing world, the heroes of yesterday become a political embarrassment to the leaders of today. The banner of the Follonsby lodge, Wardley, which featured Lenin among others, was made during a period of intense industrial and political struggle between the miners and coalowners of the north east in the early 1920s. Later, the revolutionaries were quietly painted off, and by 1947 Lenin, James Connolly and George Harvey had been replaced on the banner by union officials, A. Joyce and T. Smith.

In some lodges, the banner portrait has become a

question of seniority, president and secretary automatically being accorded the honour as they assume office, their predecessors being painted out to make way for the new officials. Local 'infighting' for such privilege has not been unknown. Havelock Wilson commented on this in 1889.

> When a branch decided to have a new banner it was well understood that the expenses for the making of the banner would be defrayed by voluntary subscriptions of the members of the branch and a banner fund would be started, but if the local committee by oversight or other want of thought had failed to have the portrait of the local secretary or other prominent members of the branch included in the portrait gallery, then the banner fund would die a natural death, and eventually the cost of the banner would have to be defrayed from the funds of the union. I think at one time we had some seventy banners each costing from £25 up to £80. The cost would largely depend on the number of portraits that would have to appear to meet aspirations.

The selection of the man or men to be portrayed on the branch or lodge banner is usually decided at a full meeting and represents the sincere choice of the men. The subjects are not always famous men but are assuredly leaders who enjoy the respect and trust of the men. The unassuming portrait on the Dean and Chapter lodge banner is such an example. Billy Todd was a Communist miner victimised in the 1930s for his activities on behalf of the miners. During the war he was reinstated on the direct intervention of Ernie Bevin who was at the time Minister of Labour. Todd was elected lodge secretary and eventually to the executive committee of the National Union of Mineworkers. Twenty-five years after his death, the last secretary of the now closed Dean and Chapter lodge recalled Todd as 'a great fighter for the working class'. Such men as Todd, Hardie, Cook and scores of agents and officials are folk heroes to the men of the mining villages and towns of Britain.

Incidentally, the Dean and Chapter lodge banner bears the name of Ellen Wilkinson, and this seems to be the only recognition of a woman working class leader on a union banner. The only identified woman to appear on a trade union banner is the First World War heroine, Nurse Edith Cavell, who was painted on the banner of Bowburn lodge. The artist was a trade unionist who worked at the mine as a painter, a man named Marrington who was victimised by the colliery undermanager for his efforts, taken off painting and given a lesser job. Women as workers are scarce on union banners made before the impact of the women's movement in recent years. They are more usually depicted as allegorical figures – liberty, truth, hope, justice, beauty or as symbolic figures, leading or pointing the way to a better life. Walter Crane, the great socialist artist contributed much to this romantic imagery. His 'angel of freedom', originally included in his painting *Freedom*, exhibited at the Grosvenor Gallery in 1885, was a recurring theme in his work and was freely adapted to adorn hundreds of union banners. Crane himself used the idea on his beautiful art nouveau banner for the Electrical Trades Union, commissioned in 1898. The alternative role of woman, as illustrated on the banners, was widow. Death, sickness and accidents are common scenes on the banners, a result of the terrible vulnerability of the breadwinner of any working class family. The constant fear described by the Brushmakers' Society was that 'Sickness might come at any moment, the vigorous health of youth might be shattered, the strong arm rendered weak or the skilfully trained hand lose its cunning.' The result of incapacitation could be devastating to a family living from week to week in an age before social security. Meagre savings were soon exhausted and the few possessions pawned and sold. For a craftsman, the last desperate act would be to sell his tools. The prospect then was parish relief and the degradation of the workhouse with separation and ruin of family life. Even the ultimate escape, death, was not without the prospect of the final humiliation of a pauper's funeral. Burial clubs, sick clubs and friendly societies abounded in Victorian Britain and the trade unions made benefit a key part of their structure and function. 'We care for our widows and orphans' became the watchword of the large craft unions and banners were adorned with those strange romantic Victorian graveside scenes, wreaths, sickbeds and widows. Against the perils of accident and sickness the unions offered small but regular weekly payments to alleviate the worst effects of poverty. In the event of the death of a member or his wife, a cash payment guaranteed a respectable burial. This concern for the 'benefits' of trade unionism led to the jealous preservation of union funds; they were not to be squandered on reckless strikes or attacking the employers. As a result, the craft unions degenerated into sick and burial societies, referred to disparagingly by the new unions as 'coffin clubs'.

'Accident' banners were to be found mostly in the dangerous trades, such as mining, building and transport, and depicted harrowing scenes of industrial injury plus the security offered by the £100 disablement benefit. This was not enough to keep a man for life, but it was a huge sum to a worker earning 20s. a week, and was the promise of a meaningful life. Even in 1907 the Amalgamated Society of Railway Servants claimed that 100,000 of their members worked for 20s. a week or less. The disablement lump sum was a strong selling point for any union organising men in heavy industry. To a railway worker, miner or bricklayer who lost a limb and would never be able to follow his trade again, £100 would establish him in his own small shop where he could work with his family and lead an independent life. The General Railway Workers' Union was formed in 1890 to cater for the casual railway labourers and others who had no place in the

Amalgamated Society of Railway Servants with its high contribution of 5d. a week. Nevertheless, benefits were still a part of the security offered. The Stratford branch banner of the GRWU in 1890 was captioned 'Platelayers' work and its dangers' and showed men working on a section of track with an approaching train in the background. Early transport unions, like the National Union of Vehicle Workers, portrayed the hazards of wheels loosening from carts. Many of the banners were painted with cameos following a story through, showing a member in hospital being visited by branch officers wearing their regalia sashes, union legal representatives fighting his case in court (where the verdict was always for the plaintiff) and finally, in fatal cases, branch officials bringing money and sympathy to the widow and orphan. The establishment of an Orphan Fund by the Amalgamated Society of Railway Servants resulted in innumerable banners depicting widow and orphan receiving trade union sympathy at the graveside or financial assistance at home. In 1882 the union was presented with a collie dog named Help, who with his collecting box was to raise over £1,000 for the orphans of railwaymen. His portrait appeared on the Stockton branch banner, and doubtless some others, the first animal to achieve such recognition. It was not until the founding of the Welfare State by the 1945 Labour government that sickness, death and injury-benefit imagery finally disappeared from the banners of British trade unionists.

From providing a decent burial to turning out in force with the union banner for a burial was a natural progression. During the 1890s, when any funeral was attended with rather more pomp and pageantry than could be afforded, burying members with full union honours became a widespread practice. For a leading figure not only would the branch officials be present with sashes and banner, but other nearby unions would be called upon to take part in the ceremony. Bands were hired and the cost to a union of burying a member at times far exceeded the amount given to the widow. The tradition was strong among the seamen and the dockers of London. For a popular member, the cortège would make its way past the dock or depot where he worked, in final farewell *en route* to the burial. After the funeral, it was not unknown for the procession to include a stop at a pub on the way back to the union office for a last drink to the memory of their brother. When Harry Gosling, a waterman, founder of the International Transport Federation and first president of the Transport and General Workers' Union, died in 1931, his body lay in state at Transport House, the hall hung with banners of the Amalgamated Society of Watermen and Lightermen and the new banners of the TGWU, the coffin draped with the shroud of the International Transport Federation. The tradition quietly declined as the vogue for elaborate funerals passed from fashion. When the Leeds Trades Council unveiled a memorial to the great trade unionist and labour leader, Tom Mann (1856-1941), in 1970, only four trade union banners were unfurled at the chapel.

Perhaps the earliest connection of trade union banners with the 'death of a brother' is found among the miners, where work and death are close companions. There is reference from 1832 to a meeting of miners bearing banners, 'one of them surrounded with a border of crape in reference to the death of a person at the colliery to which it belonged'. This method of marking the death of a comrade killed at the colliery during the past year is continued to this day. It is a reminder of the dreadful dangers of mining that scarcely a gala is held without at least one banner passing by, dressed with black. At the funerals of David Gareth Jones and Joe Green, both miners killed on the picket lines during the 1984-5 strike, the processions of mourners were headed by the black draped banners of the lodges of the victims.

In the history of trade unionism, there have been no greater banner bearers than the miners. For a century, gala days offered vast parades of bands and banners presenting a spectacle to be remembered for ever by those who took part or witnessed the processions. Born out of long struggle against rapacious coalowners, wholesale evictions, meetings broken up by police and troops, years of terrible poverty and the dreadful toll of life in the pits, the banner became a symbol and a rallying point for an entire community. With the rundown of the industry during the past twenty years, it is not uncommon to see women weep as the lodge banner is carried in a gala for the last time. It is a remarkable tribute to the quality of the miners that the mottoes, slogans and illustrations on their banners show no traces of hatred. Sorrow, toil, the brotherhood of man, the need for change, all are illustrated in vivid form, but there is not a banner which expresses vindictiveness.

To give accurate figures for the number of banners assembled at the Durham Gala in the early years is not really possible. One local newspaper report of the second Gala in 1872 put the number at a hundred and described the occasion as

> A magnificent display of bands of music and emblazoned banners. The latter indeed were specially rich in material and almost faultless in design . . . arranged on the outskirts of the great crowd each seemed to form as great an attraction to the visitors as the platform itself. In fact, the vast concourse appeared at a distance to be split up into nearly one hundred great meetings of which the colour of each colliery formed the centre.

The report continued, 'Each banner was a lecture in itself and might have furnished applicable subjects for a hundred discourses on the principles and utility of trade unions.'

Even as recently as 1961, one hundred banners are positively identified as being paraded at the gala. Since then, the number of banners has declined in direct proportion to pit closures, the number carried in 1970 having dwindled to thirty-two. In 1985, during the great strike in defence of jobs in the industry, the number of banners rose a little, though this time the number was augmented by the banners of Constituency Labour Parties and women's support groups. The actual number of Durham Area lodge banners was down to fifteen. Soon, the number of collieries left working in the Durham coalfield will be no more than eight, and the days of the big meeting remaining true to the name must be nearly at an end. Nevertheless, even in the declining years, the banners like those of a century ago have remained linked in their imagery to the ideals of trade unionism and work in the industry. At the 1969 gala I recall the Medomsley banner featured a huge lump of coal and sixteen illustrations of its uses. Eden lodge still used a Tutill design dating from the 1870s with a sickbed scene and a surround of romantic figures. Craghead lodge bore a splendid painting of Durham Cathedral backed by portraits of Clem Attlee, Arthur Horner and Nye Bevan. Ashbourne lodge showed an 'angel of freedom' handing a miner a key labelled 'Trade unionism, the key to economic emancipation'. The banner of the National Association of Colliery Overmen, Deputies and Shotfirers carried a painting of the Sam Watson Rest Home, and many banners featured aged miners' homes, convalescent homes and miners' welfares. 'The last good morning' appeared on more than one banner, a poignant picture of a miner leaving his home for the pit, never to return. A number of banners commemorated nationalisation, the 'dawn of a new era'. Possibly the most appropriate was that of Hamsterely Colliery lodge, which showed an old miner with pick and Davy lamp pointing to a modern colliery and saying to a young miner with a pneumatic drill, 'Now it's up to you.' As the collieries close, the banners are sometimes passed to another lodge and overpainted with a new name. In the post-war years, many were taken to Redhill, the Durham Area headquarters, where they were consigned to lie in basement darkness, unseen witness to the heroism and tenacity of a generation of miners. Happily, most are now lodged in a new home, at Beamish, North of England Open Air Museum, where they will be seen by hundreds of thousands of visitors in the years ahead.

As the fashion of banner bearing grew during the developing years of trade unionism, the desire of every branch to possess a magnificent silk banner to rally the members was not without its problems, for the cost was high and the money had to be found by the members themselves. This practice dates from early union history. In June 1838 at a meeting of the United Society of Boilermakers, held at the Preston Arms, Liverpool, the London No.1 branch was called to task for spending the general fund to purchase a banner, and were ordered to refund the cost out of their private purses. The tradition of making the individual branches and districts responsible for providing their own banners fortunately prevails in

the majority of the unions. It is this local autonomy which has created the diverse and richly illustrated record of trade union history they provide. The slogans, mottoes and illustrations are as varied as the branches themselves. In the few instances where trade unions have accepted national responsibility for banner design, as in the case of the twentieth-century banners of the Amalgamated Union of Engineering Workers, the Boilermakers, and the Draughtsmen's and Allied Technicians' Association, the result, no matter how commendable the design and slogans, is a standardisation which lacks the imprint of local character.

Every banner made says something of the age in which it was made and reflects the policy of the branch, district or union responsible for the selection of the designs. Ben Turner, writing of the old Weavers' Union, the General Union of Textile Workers, in 1888, unknowingly gives a perfect illustration of the historical significance of the two banners he was concerned with. He wrote

> Well do I remember the time when we tried the union to get a banner for demonstrations and an emblem for the members. I think the general executive were afraid to launch out, 'to dare something' for fear of the members complaining and criticising at the half-yearly meetings. There were some who would not see to spending a penny on what, after all, is the spice advertisement for a union. However, Messrs. Gee, Drew and myself kept at it and we got a banner made at Bradford. It is in hiding now at head office. It is not a big banner, we were limited to a few pounds-worth of banner. I remember the lines we had on it, I was much acquainted with the system that happened in weaving places where the women got longer warps and more picks per inch than paid for, and sometimes fines took part of their wages. So I wrote on the banner the lines: 'Let our warps be straight/Our picks be true/The prices just/ And paid when due'.

Just before the First World War a new banner was purchased for the union, in Turner's words 'bigger, nobler and more attractive'. This banner depicted a man and a woman textile worker shaking hands, with another verse by Ben Turner:

> The world is for the workers
> We mean to have it too
> Unite ye working comrades
> And claim what is your due.

The first banner of 1888 expressed the hope of the poor weavers for a fair deal from their wily masters. By 1915 the slogan is no longer a plea for fair play from the exploiters but a claim for the expropriation of the employing class. Both verses represent the objectives of the union at the time they were made; in 1888, reform, by 1915, control. The usual procedure, once the decision to purchase a banner had been taken, was to form a banner committee and launch a banner fund. For the branches and lodges of the better-off craft unions this often meant no more than imposing a levy on the members, who were eager to emulate their brothers of other branches who already possessed a splendid and necessary symbol of their craft. For the new unions of unskilled and semi-skilled workers whose members were already hard pressed to spare the few coppers' weekly contribution of union dues, other means had to be devised. Likewise during the years of depression, between 1890 and 1930, the members had to look beyond the membership to raise the £30 to £80 required for a suitable banner. In 1913 the Nine Elms branch of the National Union of Railwaymen raised their fund by the sale of scent cards. In 1920 the Southall branch of the Associated Society of Locomotive Engineers and Firemen bought their banner by selling fish. The drivers would buy boxes of fish at Grimsby and bring them on the footplate to London where the fish was sold and the proceeds contributed to the banner fund. Most trade union banners appear to have been purchased by money raised from raffles. The National Amalgamated Workers' Union minute book of 1919-1923 gives a typical account of the long and difficult task of raising the money to buy the Peterborough district banner from Tutill's. The proposal for a banner was first put to the branch on 23 August 1919. A banner committee was formed and the matter was raised by the secretaries of the local branches. By July 1920 a watch committee was considered necessary to keep an eye on the growing fund. In September of that year the committee agreed on the size of the banner, eleven by nine feet (3.40 x 2.70 m), and confirmed the slogans, 'The security of all depends on the unity of each' and 'The cause of labour is the hope of the world'. Evidently, discussion on the design continued, for a meeting on 16 October endorsed some alterations to the design. By March 1921 the members decided on a competition, based on guessing the finalists of the English Cup, and offered a first prize of one ton of coal. It was proposed and seconded that one hundred books, each with twenty-eight tickets, should be purchased and sold at 3d. each. On 2 April there was a lengthy debate on placing the final order and whether to have a waterproof cover at an extra cost of 10s. 6d. At the same time it was agreed that every branch borrowing the district banner should pay 5s. plus expenses of transport. It was agreed that the banner should be insured, and the money for the purchase of the banner was borrowed from the Peterborough branch; the members decided that the banner should be unfurled at Whittlesea at the earliest date possible. On 9 July 1921 the draw was held at the Labour Party rooms, the total raised after expenses being £9. 11s. 4½d. The banner, duly unfurled, must have proved difficult to carry, for at a meeting held on 15 October 1921 at the Labour Party rooms it was proposed, on expert advice, and seconded, that the banner poles should be shortened by six inches and this was carried unanimously.

December 10 came and the banner fund showed that a sum of £21. 14s. 5d. was still due to the Peterborough branch, and it was carried that a draw on the football Cup Final should be held. The minutes record the loan of the banner to various branches of the union and it was carried in the May Day demonstration of 1922. On 9 July the banner was damaged by high winds, which caused considerable consternation, and a letter was sent to Tutill's regarding the endurance of silk. In the meantime the banner was repaired free of charge by a local man, J. Barrett, a tailor, and it was agreed that his generosity should be recognised by writing a letter of thanks. It was ordered that the thanks should be recorded in the minute book. In February 1923 the banner fund was still in debt to the Peterborough branch and another draw was arranged, with tickets at 2d. each. Here the account ends. If the sum seems trifling and the efforts pathetic, it should be remembered that this was a period of continuous high unemployment. The minutes record, week after week, the hardship of unemployed members, the offer to mend the boots of the children of the unemployed free of charge by handy members of the union, and the donation of £1 from the hardship fund to a member unemployed for a year, whose daughter had been sick for eleven months. In these circumstances the decision to publicly proclaim 'The cause of labour is the hope of the world' is seen as a heroic faith in the principles of trade unionism and their determination to fight the greedy system which robbed them of the fundamental right to work. The account of the struggle to purchase the banner of the Amalgamated Workers' Union has been the story of the birth of hundreds of banners. Unlike many, the banner survives and is cared for by the Peterborough District Office of the Transport and General Workers' Union. Apart from the new name, which has been overpainted, the banner is as it was the day it was bought.

1919 was a boom year for banners, the result of a new militancy which had begun in 1914 with fierce strikes of dockers and seamen. The post-war banners reflected the growing influence of syndicalist ideas, the inspiration of the Russian revolution of 1917 and the power of the Triple Alliance, the unity agreement mooted in 1914 between the miners, railwaymen and transport workers. The syndicalist ideas, of which Tom Mann was a leading exponent, found strong support among sections of the railwaymen who emblazoned their banners with demands for political and industrial action to destroy capitalism, The theme was organisation by industry, not craft, the watchword was unity and the power of the working class to withdraw their labour the key to working class power. The whole story of the period is captured on the banner of the Southend branch of the National Union of Railwaymen. The scene depicts a worker trampling poverty, symbolised by a wild boar, underfoot, as he strangles the wolf of capitalism. The struggle takes place on the threshold of the citadel of capitalism which the worker intends to take by storm. At the foot of the banner an NUR train is seen leaving the dark tunnel of 'sectionalism and craft unionism' running on the track of 'industrial unionism' to victory. The slogans shout, 'Nationalisation in the interest of all' and 'Political, industrial and economic freedom', while the sun of socialism is seen rising over the horizon. One can imagine the militant members of the branch each adding his own point to make up this amazing composite picture.

The Rickmansworth branch of the NUR devised a banner design which showed two railway workers shackled by a huge ball and chain of capitalism, and illustrating political and industrial action as the way to emancipation. The slogan reads, 'The liberation of the working class is the act of the workers themselves.' The West Ham branch of the union declared on their banner, 'Non-stop from wage slavery to industrial freedom', urging 'Comrades, courage and forward'. The influence extended to craft-proud unions such as the Associated Society of Locomotive Engineers and Firemen, whose Southall branch banner proclaimed, 'The power of unity breaks down the barriers of capitalism' and showed an alarmed board of railway directors being kicked out as a giant worker breaks through the 'barriers of capitalism'. The Southend branch of the National Union of General Workers, possibly inspired by their fellow workers on the railway, depicted a worker breaking his chains and slaying the capitalist wolf. The Tottenham branch of the union illustrated a group of workers looking to industrial organisation, political action and 'real international' as the means of achieving the cooperative commonwealth. Their slogans said, 'Producers of the nation's wealth, unite! and have your share of the world.' The many banners of the Workers' Union, just before their federation, were always militant; the Witney branch showed David, representing the workers, slaying Goliath, the giant of capitalism, with the motto 'He that would be free must strike the blow.'

The prevailing spirit of militancy saw revolutionaries painted onto the banners of mining's 'Little Moscows'. James Connolly, James Larkin, George Harvey, Karl Marx and Lenin appeared on banners, as did the hammer and sickle and the red star, emblems of the new Soviet state. In Mardy, in the Rhondda Valley, a Russian banner, a gift from Soviet miners, was used to drape the coffin at the funeral of a communist miner. The banners of dockers, railwaymen and transport workers demonstrated the unity of the Triple Alliance with representatives of the three unions depicted holding three links of a giant chain or clasping hands in a triple handshake. The Canning Town branch banner of the NUR showed the wolf of capitalism slinking away before an advancing group of miner, railwayman and docker, their arms linked together. To read the mottoes on the banners made after the First World War is to capture the flavour of the idealism and socialist aspirations of the unions at that time. Banner after banner looked to nationalisation as the road to future prosperity. The Northumberland miners at the Ashington group of collieries headed their banner with the words 'A plea for nationalisation' and showed a heroic worker with a spear of 'State control' slaying the dragon of 'profit and private ownership'. 'Public ownership', 'socialisation', 'state owned cottages', 'The wealth for the workers' are all found on banners of the period. Neither are they confined to the large industrial unions; the Shropshire branch of the National Union of Agricultural Workers urged, 'Land workers unite, you have only your chains to lose and a world to win by unity'. The South Tottenham branch of the Union of Post Office Workers echoed the marxist slogan and looked to the 'Sunshine of liberty' depicted as a world of happy children and parents housed in tidy brick suburban homes. The goal as painted on hundreds of banners was the socialist or cooperative commonwealth, where art, science and industry would flourish, a clean, planned and organised society to replace the dirty slums and prison-like factories. Of all the mottoes, 'No starving children in the board schools' used on many banners, is perhaps the most evocative of the desperate years after the First World War. The demand was for a new kind of society and, for doubters, an inspiring verse is to be found on more than one banner

> Impossible, there's no such word
> Should e'er be used by any man,
> With faith all things are possible,
> They conquer who believe they can.

This enthusiasm seems to have ended with the General Strike of 1926. Disillusionment and the struggle against massive unemployment made the years between 1926 and 1939 as unfruitful for banners as any time since 1889. It was not until the eventual 'triumph of labour' in 1945 that the same idealism produced a fresh upsurge in the demand for new banners. This time, the banners celebrated the new power of Labour government and the assured future of socialism. Nationalisation was no longer a dream, it was reality: 'The dawn of a new era' as proclaimed by Risca lodge, the acquisition of 'Our heritage' in the words of Harton and Westoe lodge. Portraits of cabinet ministers decorated the banners together with illustrations of the 'Act of Nationalisation' being handed to the miners. Many old banners which illustrated the lodge colliery had the letters NCB added to the picture of the pithead. The imagery was confident, forward looking and full of the promise of peace and socialism. New banners were ordered by engineering workers, agricultural workers, boilermakers and miners on a considerable scale. Other unions replaced some of their banners lost or destroyed during the war. Amalgamations meant new banners for new unions, although not all new unions saw the need for a banner to announce their arrival. During the 1950s banner making declined until by the late 1960s it had virtually ceased apart from the tradition maintained by the miners. Resurgence began in 1971, when the TUC organised a great march and demonstration against the Industrial Relations Bill of the Conservative government. This was the largest procession of banner bearing trade unionists to march through the streets of the capital since May Day 1926, more than 50,000 actually taking part in the march to Trafalgar Square where more than 100,000 gathered to register their protest. Hundreds of banners were carried, though not more than sixty were of the traditional kind, and many were enjoying their first airing for some years. Excluding the slogan banners, a few of the newer unions made banners especially for the occasion, although they were simple affairs compared with the others. These included the National Union of Waterworks Employees, the Association of Scientific, Technical and Managerial Staffs, the Civil Service Union, and the Association of Cinematograph, Television and Allied Technicians. Apart from the familiar banners of the miners, engineers and printers, there were some rare glimpses of the banners of the Inland Revenue Staff Federation, and the National League of the Blind. However, it was the great banners of the past that brought wonderment and admiration from the assembled onlookers, watched with the kind of awe usually accorded to parades of vintage cars or traction engines. If their style belonged to a bygone age, the messages they carried of brotherhood and unity for labour and justice were as relevant as they were on the day they were painted.

The effect was not lost on the thousands who saw, many for the first time, the full colour, dignity and pride created by these silken wonders. Many young artists were inspired to try their hand at banner painting and there has been a proliferation of new banners, especially from the 'white collar' unions. The styles vary from traditional to contemporary, but in a Britain with 4,000,000 unemployed and the 'sun of socialism', as painted on countless banners, still on the horizon, the need for workers to give expression to their hopes for a more just, peaceful and equitable society is as vital as it ever was.

THE BANNER MAKERS

The first trade union banners were simple devices painted by local signwriters, coachpainters or decorators. Occasionally a touch of professionalism appears as in the case of the Nantwich shoemakers, who in 1834 extravagantly engaged the local Herald painter, Mr Thomas Jones, to paint their banner at a cost of £25. Often, the banners were made by a member of the branch considered to have an artistic turn of hand.

There have always been a small number of home-made banners. Margaret Bondfield in her autobiography quotes a letter from the son of an old colleague who describes the making of such a banner (for the Shop Assistants' Union, King's Cross) in 1891.

> An old ticket writer was found, who for a shilling cut out the white glazed letters, which mother stitched onto a heavy red twill which made a patch of glory on high, mounted on the alder-wood poles which my father made . . .

Stories like this recur from time to time and some examples are included in this collection. The cooperative effort of the vehicle builders at Standard Triumph is a good example of a home-made banner. But these represent only a tiny percentage of the total. More than three quarters of all the trade union banners made from 1837 onwards can be attributed to a single commercial company, founded by a remarkable Victorian, George Tutill. He was born in the Yorkshire village of Howden in 1817, two years after the final defeat of Napoleon at Waterloo and two years before the English yeomanry were to cut down their fellow Englishmen at the massacre at Peterloo. His father was Thomas Tutill, an illiterate miller. Although the first trade union banner had been unfurled well before his birth, it should be remembered that even when Tutill was seventeen years old, in 1834, the martyrs of Tolpuddle were sentenced to seven years' transportation for daring to form a trade union. Yet, three years later, in 1837, at the age of twenty, young Tutill was to establish the company which was to manufacture more trade union banners than any other in the world.

Details of his life before 1837 are obscure. The business which he founded still exists, trading under the name of George Tutill Limited, in Chesham, Bucks, and in association with Turtle and Pearce Limited in Southwark, London. A former manager at Chesham was Ronald Caffyn, who has more experience in the art of making banners for trade unions than any other living man. His family has a long record of service with Tutill's, and Caffyn started work with the firm in 1931. His father, Charles Henry Caffyn, worked at Tutill's from the 1880s and actually met the founder. His mother, who had been apprenticed as a regalia apron-maker to Kennings, also came to Tutill's and later became forewoman. The story of how the young Tutill became known as the 'universal provider' of regalia for the trade unions is passed from Charles Caffyn to his son Ronald. Although the story is uncorroborated, the association of this family with the firm over the past ninety years must give considerable credibility to the account. Ronald Caffyn relates:

> George Tutill began his life as a travelling fairground showman. In those days, as in some cases to this day, it was common practice for a showman to decorate his own sideshow, caravan or roundabout, embellishing it with ornate lettering and design, which Tutill did with great style. It is also known (a fact which is substantiated) that he had a taste for good ale and was a regular frequenter of public houses. Tutill first met with trade unionists during his regular visits to public houses. He also met with the friendly societies for whom he was to produce so much work in the years to come . . . On one occasion whilst in a pub he was asked if he would paint a banner for a union which held its meeting at the inn. He accepted and the members of the branch were delighted with the result.

The astute showman immediately saw his chance to leave fairground life and set up on his own as a banner painter for the trade unions and friendly societies. The influence of fairground art on nineteenth-century banners is apparent from early paintings of fairground scenes, and later from photographs of country fairs. An oil painting of the Melton Mowbray Statute Fair at York in 1837 by John Ferneley (1815-1862) shows large canvas fascias resembling the format and style of later union banners, suspended from poles each side of a stage. Photographs taken at the St Giles' Fair, Oxford, in the 1890s show an even stronger resemblance to banner art and a cameo painting of the fascia to Rephs' waxworks at the fair in 1895 is virtually identical to a Tutill painting on a National Union of General Workers' banner, thirty years later.

David slaying Goliath, detail from the fascia to Rephs' waxworks and exhibition of fine art, 1895. Note the similarity of the cameo to the detail from a Tutill banner on page 130.

The fascia to Dav's menagerie at the St Giles fair, 1895. The format of the painted canvasses closely resembles the style of union banners. Note the circular cameos at the top of the canvasses.

In the 1830s, and well into the twentieth century, it was customary for the unions to meet in public houses. Local authorities and clergy were rarely sympathetic to trade unions, and municipal offices and village halls were seldom available to them for meetings. A room at the local inn, the traditional rendezvous of working men, provided the only real alternative. This suited the landlord who let the room free and in return enjoyed the regular custom of the members. The pubs were also used as 'call houses' by journeymen on the tramp, who would go there to meet their brothers of the local society and seek details of work available in the village or town. Tutill no doubt grasped that trade unionism was growing. The facts of which we can be certain are these: Tutill always claimed to have set up his business in 1837. In

1847 a painting by a G. Tutill entitled *Scarborough Castle* was exhibited at the Royal Academy. By 1857 he was living at 8 Angel Terrace, St Peter's Street, Islington, and was well on the road to success. By 1859, possibly a little earlier, his banner-making business was installed in splendid and spacious premises at 83 City Road, the building having been designed specifically for the purpose. Three galleries, with natural light from a glass roof, provided ideal studios for the artist. In addition, there was ample room for the other processes involved in complete manufacture. By 1860 he had moved to 14 Douglas Road, Canonbury, a mark of middle class achievement. In no more than twenty years of commercial art on behalf of the social movements of Victorian England he had become a

Boxers await challenges at the St Giles fair, 1898, in front of fascias that reflect the fairground origins of trade union banner art.

wealthy man. To achieve this he had raised banner making from a local signwriters's job to a production line flow that would have pleased Henry Ford.

All Tutill's banners were made of pure silk and he was influenced in establishing his business in East London by the proximity of the colony of silkweavers in Spitalfields and Bethnal Green. The weavers were descended from an unbroken line of Huguenots who came to live in Canterbury and Spitalfields after the revocation of the Edict of Nantes. In the evidence taken before a committee of the House of Commons on the silk trade in 1831, the population of Spitalfields, Bethnal Green, Mile End and Newtown was given as 100,000, of whom 50,000 were entirely dependent on silk manufacture. It was estimated that there were 17,000 looms in operation. For most of the weavers it was a miserable life of poverty. In the first quarter of the nineteenth century, according to evidence contained in parliamentary reports, the average weekly earnings did not exeed 5s. if periods of waiting were taken into account. Originally, Tutill had purchased his silk lengths from the Spitalfields weavers. For banners requiring a woven patterned background he imported the squares from France. Unable to control the quality of the silk or weave the design of his choice, and seeking greater control of production, he introduced hand looms into the new premises in the 1860s.

On 6 July 1861 Tutill took out a patent for 'treating materials for the manufacture of banners and flags'. The invention was contrived to give flexibility and durability to the pictorial centre of the banners in which oil colours were applied to the silk. The patent system employed was to coat the silk with a thin solution of india rubber. When this coating had dried, either in a heated chamber or by oxidization, a second coat, combined with linseed oil, was applied. The paint then used for the painting was mixed with old oil, or oil that had been exposed to the effect of the atmosphere for some time. The paint thus dried quickly, enabling the many colours to be applied faster, and at the same time rendered the colour more pliant, flexible and elastic, so that the paint would not peel from the banner. Unsophisticated as the method was, it worked.One hundred years later the colours are as pliant and bright as the day they were painted if the banners have been stored in reasonable conditions.

Tutill was now able to advertise 'Patent india rubber pure silk banners' and denounce his competitors whose products had 'that heavy boardy thickness of the painted parts so noticeable in the productions of "banner amateurs"'! This comment seems to have been directed at William Elam, a banner painter of 257 Hackney Road, London, who made his banners of the twilled silk which Tutill so despised. At Tutill's manufactory in City Road, the actual painting of the illustrations on the banners was only a part of the total production. His assembly line began with a hank of raw silk. It was dyed, wound and warped. It then had to be woven into pieces up to twelve feet wide. Tutill offered two types of banners, woven and non-woven. For the cheaper non-woven banners, the decorative surround to the centre panel would be painted by hand in gold or silver on plain silk. Under Tutill's rationalised system of production, this would be the work of a specialist, a 'cornerman'. For the more expensive and better quality banners, the decorative surround would be woven into the silk whilst on the loom. The centre paintings were the work of a team of highly skilled artists, again specialists. One artist would paint the portraits of the trade union leaders, MPs and other public figures who adorned so many of the banners at the end of the nineteenth century. Another would specialise in painting technical scenes form the widely differing industries and crafts featured on the union banners. Other general artists would handle the landscapes, crowd scenes, emblems, badges and the like. Finally, a signwriter would paint in the title of the lodge or branch and the inevitable motto or slogan. The banner would be supplied complete with twelve-foot stained and polished carrying poles, made of straight-grained Douglas pine and fitted with brass ferrules and ornamented spearheads. The cross pole would be silvered and the banner trimmed and tasselled, fitted with silk cords and guide tapes. The tapes were secured to the banner by brass discs, bearing the inscription 'George Tutill . . . Sole manufacturer of patent banners'. The banner was sent to the purchaser (with free fire insurance for a year) wrapped in a waterproof cover and housed in a magnificent 4.27 metres long wooden box.

For the actual painting the silk would be stretched taut on a wooden frame and inclined forward towards the artist so that any splashes of colour would fall to the floor and not upon the banner. Pure silk has amazing strength and when stretched upon the frame is as taut as a drum. Tutill himself has left an amusing anecdote illustrating the powers of resistance of his silk banners. Showing a prospective customer around his gallery, Tutill remarked, 'You might throw yourself bodily against it and it would not break.' The visitor without more ado took him at his word. He was painfully surprised a moment later to find himself lying on the floor six feet from the banner! Tutill made full use of a number of basic designs which could be offered at low cost although, as he pointed out, no two banners were ever identical. He contrived designs which would serve equally well for a trade union or a temperance society. As on the banner of the Witney branch of the Workers' Union, David slaying Goliath might carry a militant trade union caption. Given the motto 'England sober, is England free', David portrayed total abstinence slaying the giant of intemperance. Similarly, all the popular emblems of truth, hope, justice, the 'all-seeing eye' and every kind of medieval symbol Tutill could find were cleverly woven into composite designs and spurious coats of arms ready for any society requiring instant dignity and status. This explains why the design of the Workers' Union banner (illustrated on cover) bears a strong similarity to the banner of the Order of True Ivorites, made in 1896. The dexter hand and heart, widely used as a symbol by the Oddfellows, the hand indicating friendship, the heart love, and the two combined truth, is also found on the banner of the Flax Dressers' Trade and Benevolent Trade Union. This is almost certainly because Tutill's suggested it as an additional and seemingly appropriate embellishment to the design. Standard designs would be painted by the artists on a piece-work basis, though this was not always popular. One new artist was given a Sunday school banner to paint, depicting Jesus with a flock of sheep. After working out the illustration, he walked out, never to return, with the comment, 'What, paint Jesus Christ and a flock of bleeding sheep for a quid? Not likely.'

Another ready source of imagery for the Tutill business was the cartoons of Walter Crane (1845-1915). Already famous as an illustrator and pre-Raphaelite artist when he was converted to socialism in 1884, Crane gave freely of his talents to the cause of labour to become the most influential of British artists in shaping the popular iconography of trade unionism. Crane himself designed few banners, among them works for the Electrical Trades Union, the Social Democratic Federation, the National Federation of Women Workers, the Irish Nationalists and, it is said, the agricultural workers, although this banner remains unidentified. However, it was his cartoons, drawings made for socialist journals, *Justice*, *Clarion*, *Commonweal* and *Labour Leader* that were to become a standard reference for Tutill banners for forty years or more. Hundreds of banners were based on his cartoons, 'The International Solidarity of Labour' (1889), 'The Triumph of Labour' (1891), 'The Workers' Maypole' (1894) and 'A Garland for May Day' (1895). Many more were inspired by his 'Angel of Freedom', derived from his original oil painting, *Freedom*, exhibited at the Grosvenor Gallery in 1885. Described by Crane as a 'vision breaking into the sunshine of spring', the winged female figure was freely interpreted on the banners as a vision leading to the sunshine of socialism. Leaves from Crane's *Cartoons for the Cause*, issued as a 'Souvenir of the International Socialist Workers and Trades Union Congress' in 1896, were to remain pinned on the walls of Tutill's studio until 1940.

Tutill's activities at City Road were not confined to trade union banners. Regalia for Oddfellows, Comical Fellows, Free Gardeners, Masons, Church Sunday schools, Bands of Hope, Temperance Societies, Rechabites, Orange lodges and every kind of friendly society were manufactured to order. Satin sashes, printed emblems, aprons, collars, regalia cases, caps, certificates, medals, chains, horns, girdles and even robes and false beards for the United Ancient Order of Druids, supplied a seemingly insatiable demand.

With business flourishing Tutill continued to prosper, and in 1871 he moved his home to an imposing residence, the Red House, Upton Lane, West Ham. This fine house was built shortly before 1762 and had been inhabited by Isaac Blijdestijn, the son of a Dutch merchant. Tutill was to live there with his wife, Elizabeth and their only child, his daughter Georgina, until his death in 1887. The armorial of a glass fanlight over the door of the main entrance is that of Tutill, also the paintings on the doors and the bronze window decorations.

Seeking to improve the quality of his silk banners and to speed production, Tutill installed a Jacquard loom early in the 1880s. This was the invention of Joseph Marie Jacquard, a Frenchman, who perfected the loom in 1801. But not until 1820 were a few Jacquard looms smuggled into England and secretly set up. In spite of initial opposition they soon came into general use, especially for hand looms and silk pattern weaving. They greatly simplified the weaver's work and could be programmed to produce intricate ornamental designs. On the earlier looms the warp had to be raised and lowered by hand, but the Jacquard could be made to govern all the operations except throwing the shuttle and actuating the lever by which it was put into operation. The Jacquard apparatus, which may be described as a punch-card system, selected the warp threads to be raised to produce the pattern and change the shuttle boxes in correct succession. It gave rise to a prosperous class of craftsmen in Spitalfields; Jacquard machinists, designers, draughtsmen and cardcutters were all to be found within walking distance of Tutill's premises. Typically on the grand scale, Tutill's Jacquard loom was claimed to be the largest in the world when installed. Specially designed and built for him in Bethnal Green by the firm of Maddox, it was capable of weaving a pattern nine feet wide and repeating every nine feet. From the colony of silkweavers, Tutill was fortunate to obtain the services of Frederick Owers, born in 1847, a master craftsman who had begun his working life picking and winding at Braintree, also a silk-weaving district. Owers, a superb craftsman, claimed to be one of the first men to weave a trade union banner, and in an interview with a newspaper reporter he showed a remnant of a hand-woven trade union banner on which he had set a record of silk throwing never likely to be equalled. The usual 'throw' of the shuttle is across a warp of 16.5 to 71.1 centimetres and the average number of threads in the warp is 4,000. For this banner Owers had to make a throw of 289.6 centimetres and the number of threads he had to keep straight was 36,000! This remarkable man was still weaving and teaching at the age of eighty-eight, his eyesight still perfect. It was Fred Owers's brother, James, who installed the Jacquard loom for Tutill. With the new programmed loom they were able to produce the Renaissance-style woven pattern that is to be found on so many of the surviving banners from that period.

Tutill seems to have been the very essence of the successful Victorian businessman: self-made, creative, inventive and boldly keeping pace with the expansion of industrial capitalism at home and abroad. He soon developed a flourishing export business. While the wealthy white man bore his burdens with some fortitude in the remote colonies, the same Imperial dedication did not always inspire the poor white immigrants who now slaved for wages in different climes. They carried with them the experience of organisation gained from trade union membership in Britain. Very soon they needed banners to proclaim themselves and the grand old Victorian provider was quick to oblige, packing them in tin-lined banner boxes to withstand the journey and the dangers of strange climates. In the Tutill catalogue of 1895, it is stated that he was exporting banners to Australia, New Zealand, South Africa, Canada and, rather vaguely, 'to the remotest parts of the civilised world'. Tutill won the highest award, a gold medal, and a special commendation at the Sydney Exhibition of 1879. He also took first prizes at exhibitions in Brisbane in 1880, Melbourne in 1881 and Adelaide in 1882. He took the opportunity of journeying to Australia for the occasion of the Melbourne exhibition, sailing on the *Garonne* of the Orient Line and combining his business trip with a tour which included New Zealand, Hawaii, New York, San Francisco, Salt Lake City and Chicago. He was obviously missed by his drinking companions at the Star public house in City Road and a printed piece of verse, evidently compiled by one of them, survives to commemorate the voyage. It is headed 'Song, composed in celebration of the safe return of Mr. George Tutill from his Antipodean and Transatlantic Peregrinations, 1881'. The verse refers to the exhibition, 'the flags and choice regalia, quite a masterpiece of heraldry, 'twas far above all rivalry' and runs to 125 lines.

Although in half a century Tutill made more trade union banners than anyone else, there is nothing to suggest that he shared the political or social persuasions of the unions. Indeed, it is ironic that this story of popular socialism should centre on so uncompromising a capitalist. He ran a non-union shop while advertising himself as 'Brother George Tutill' and it was not until 1934, during the manufacture of a centenary banner to commemorate the transportation of the Tolpuddle Martyrs, that a vigilant official of the Agricultural Workers' Union asked to see the union cards! The staff were only then enrolled into a local branch of the National Union of Tailors and Garment Workers, their dues being paid by the company. He also obtained a great deal of business from the temperance movement, but he was certainly not teetotal. He is said to have kept two barrels in his office, one filled with whisky for the drinkers, the other with port for the non-drinkers.

He was evidently on friendly terms with most of the trade union leaders of his day and there were many meetings in his office to discuss the order of a new banner. The tradition continued after his death when his son-in-law, H.W.E. Storey, inherited most of the company. The dockers' leaders were frequent visitors to the firm after the 1889 struggle, and a photograph of Tom Mann and Ben Tillett as well as a photograph of the Great Dock Strike committee, signed by them all, hung in the office until 1940.

George Tutill was a meticulous artist and business administrator. He kept long-hand records of all his correspondence from 1840 onwards. These were kept in fast-bound volumes, stored in the vaults of 83 City Road. Later he used to photograph every banner made by the company, building up a complete visual record of his work. This task was to become the responsibility of Charles Caffyn, pioneer of micro-photography. The entire collection of records and glass negatives (with the exception of fifteen boxes of negatives, twelve boxes of which were only re-discovered in 1985) was lost when the building was totally destroyed during the Nazi blitz in 1940. It is a tragedy for Labour historians that this unique record of a century of work for the trade unions should be lost forever. Ronald Caffyn himself can remember seeing correspondence with unions going back to the 1840s. The giant Jacquard loom was removed to the firm of silkweavers, F. Warner & Sons, at Braintree in 1939 for safekeeping. After the war Warners sought to return the loom to Tutills, but as their premises at City Road were destroyed they did not have room to accommodate it. The loom was offered to the Science Museum, which declined it, and in 1965 it was dismantled and destroyed. Fortunately, a few of Tutill's illustrated catalogues have survived. Of two in my possession, one was printed in 1895, the other in 1930. The earlier catalogue is a foolscap-size book running to 168 illustrated pages, while the 1930 edition is a mere booklet of five inches by four inches and a hundred pages shorter.

The two catalogues emphasise the sharp decline in banner making from the boom decade at the end of the last century to the demoralisation of trade unionism that followed the General Strike. Apart from the difference in size, the most striking feature is the similarity of designs in both brochures. In many instances standard designs being offered in the 1890s were still available in 1930. This explains why so many trade unionists are misled into believing that their banners are much older than is so. Victorian-styled figures were often painted onto union banners well after the close of the Victorian era. It is only on the banners made to the specific requirements of a union that dating becomes an easier task. Cost comparison is interesting for it shows little difference in the cost of banner making over the thirty-five years between 1895 and 1930. In 1895 a twelve by eleven feet (3.70 x 3.40 m) woven and painted banner cost a basic 32 guineas. Added to this would be the cost of poles, carrying harness, cords and banner box. Allowing for further charges for portraits or specialised industrial scenes, the total would still have been under £55. By 1930 the cost of a similar banner had risen to only £70. Costs have escalated rapidly during the last fifty years, though direct comparison is not possible. Today, an embroidered banner of the type Tutill's made for sixty years is simply not obtainable.

Apart from the decline in the market, little seems to have changed at Tutill's City Road 'manufactory' in the years between the two catalogues. The 1930 edition still advertised 'silk woven by practical workmen on the largest and finest silk looms in the world'. The emphasis is still on quality, fair trading and the ever-open invitation to 'inspect the making of banners in all stages of production'. The 1930 catalogue is written as if George Tutill were still alive and says, 'I am a silk manufacturer as well as an artist', and that the whole process of manufacture is 'under my personal supervision'. Testimonial letters were still being addressed to 'Dear Mr Tutill' in 1947 although he had been dead for sixty years. Even today, some trade unionists will tell you that their banner was made by Mr Tutill after the Second World War. In fact, Tutill died on 17 February 1887 at his home in West Ham, the business passing to his daughter and his son-in-law. The line of Tutill and the reign of the banner king ended there. He was an extraordinary man, who had been in the right place at the right time. At an early age he grasped the possibilities associated with the social and political reform movements of Victorian Britain. He understood the British addiction to societies, and the desire of ordinary men for colour and a sense of dignity and purpose in their lives. He combined the rare dual qualities of natural artistic ability and business acumen. Above all, he was a showman.

The business continued and prospered during the boom decade of the nineties. In the twentieth century, demand declined until after the First World War, when there was an upsurge in trade union banner making as the heroes fought a further war against employers. Following the General Strike and the eventual defeat of the miners by the government and coalowners, the demand for banners dropped away and did not rise again until 1947. In the flush of victory, the miners and agricultural workers in particular reorganised and equipped themselves with many splendid banners in traditional style. The demand dwindled after that, and in 1967, for the first time in 130 years, not a single trade union banner was made by George Tutill's.

Since 1945 there have been a number of attempts by artists who are also socialists to establish small banner-making companies working for the wider labour movement. In 1945 the Co-operative Art Service was formed by three designers, Harry Mattey, George Mayhew and Bill Judge. They made a number of banners during the short revival after the Second World War, their banners usually readily identified by the use of silk-screen printing for part, or all of the design. Materials were difficult to obtain in the post-war years and though the banners were of sound design, they were of poor quality. The co-partnership did not survive long and was dissolved in 1954. In 1956 a company known as Mountain and Molehill was formed by two socialists, Ken Sprague and Ray Bernard, to design and produce publicity material for the trade unions. The partnership enjoyed some success, and in 1960 they actively sought orders for the manufacture of trade union banners. A small number were produced, the designs mainly the work of Ken Sprague, and the banners sewn and made up by a subcontract arrangement with skilled outworkers. Three banners made by Mountain and Molehill are of particular interest: the ETU banner, which is a fine example of Sprague's powerful style, and the banners of the old Amalgamated Union of Foundry Workers and the Glasgow branch of the Union of Post Office Workers. The Foundry Workers' banner carries the design (two hands moulding a world) reproduced on the gold medal presented to the world's first space traveller, Major Yuri Gagarin, by the union in 1961. Gagarin was a former foundry worker and the banner design was based on the medal design, which was also the work of Sprague. The Union of Post Office Workers' banner was carried in the Glasgow May Day parade for the first time in 1961 and is in traditional style, illustrating the wide range of Post Office work: the telephonist, the postman, the telegraphist, the postman, higher grade, the Postal and Telegraph Office and the cleaner. It carries the UPW badge, the caduceus of Mercury, and is hand embroidered in heavy gold silk thread. However, too few unions could be persuaded of the value of parading a colour and the hoped-for banner department never materialised. The company was finally wound up in 1979.

The most successful of the resurgent banner companies is undoubtedly Chippenham Designs. Founded by John Midgley in 1969, the firm began work in an artists' cooperative in Kilburn, later moving to Willesden and now housed in a modern building in Norfolk where they have been since 1980. A one-hundred-percent trade union firm, Chippenham are constantly working on banners for the labour movement, both in the traditional and modern style. Unlike older commercial banner-making companies, Chippenham work solely for the wider labour movement and it is typical of the commitment of the firm that the staff contributed towards the cost of the banner for the Leicestershire miners during the 1984-5 strike.

Old established companies like Turtle and Pearce and Toye, Kenning and Spencer continue to make the occasional trade union banner, usually in the traditional style, employing methods similar to those used by Tutill's a century ago. If the banners they make cost more than those produced by their newer rivals, their defence is that their banners have a longer life.

Around the country, individual artists and small cooperative groups are working producing banners, each in their own style, breaking the conformity of design imposed by the near monopoly of trade union banner making held by Tutill's for a hundred years. Talented artists like Ken Sprague, Conrad Atkinson and Andrew Turner have all made valuable contributions to the banner art of the last decade. Other workshops, including Corby Community Arts, Banner Arts and Campbell Design have helped to broaden the variety of materials used, change the methods of manufacture and introduce an exciting variety of style to modern banner making.

To witness a mass procession of trade unionists today is to see a new idealism reflected in the imagery of an old tradition. Black workers, women workers and the new technology of industry feature large in the painted symbolism. Women stand shoulder to shoulder with men, black hands clasp white hands, equality is given a new expression, new mottoes mingle with the old in unity and working class solidarity. Despite all the modern means of electronic communication, there is still nothing to move the heart and stir the pride like the proud rippling of a painted sail against the wind, borne aloft by the hands of working people, marching for the great and lasting cause of labour, 'the hope of the world'.

BRO. GEORGE TUTILL,

𝕬rtistic 𝕭anner 𝕻ainter,

83, CITY ROAD, LONDON,

MANUFACTURER OF THE

PATENT ∗ INDIARUBBER ∗ SILK ∗ BANNERS,

WITHOUT SEAMS; ALSO

PATENT WOVEN BANNERS,

WITH HANDSOME ORNAMENTAL SCROLLS WOVEN IN THE SILK.

(Any Designs Painted in Centre, both sides.)

For Prices and Particulars see Illustrated Catalogue, which will be sent you upon application to above address.

Also Manufacturer of every description of

PERSONAL REGALIA FOR ALL SOCIETIES

AT REASONABLE PRICES.

SASHES, APRONS, COLLARS, &c.,

Supplied from Stock per return, or made to order.

Samples sent Carriage Free, upon receipt of order bearing Seal.

Also Manufacturer of all kinds of

STATIONERY FOR SOCIETIES' USE.

Books, Summonses, Cards,

CERTIFICATES, ENVELOPES, NOTE PAPER, &c.,

ALL GOODS SENT CARRIAGE PAID.

Any article sent per return, on receipt of Stamps or Post Office Order, or through the Lodge Secretary, with Order bearing the Official Seal.

Cheques crossed Bank of England. Post Office Orders made payable at General Post Office, E.C.

THE BANNER MAKERS

The front cover of the 1895 Tutill
catalogue showing the various aspects
of banner making at the famous City
Road manufactory.

Winding bobbins ready for the looms. The fibre is cotton, which was woven with silk to make silk-shot cotton for the regalia sashes so popular with trade union officials of the late nineteenth century.

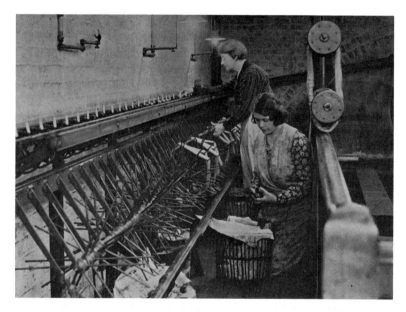

Winding off skeins of silk ready for the warp. For regalia sashes, the weft was cotton and the warp silk.

James Owers, one of the two brothers employed to install the specially constructed looms at 83 City Road.

GEORGE TUTILL,
83, CITY ROAD, LONDON.

INVENTOR AND SOLE PATENTEE
OF THE
MAGNIFICENT WOVEN BANNERS
With Scroll and Ornamental designs woven in the silk, and APPROPRIATE PAINTINGS ON
BOTH SIDES to order,

AND MANUFACTURER OF THE
PATENT INDIARUBBER SILK (in One Piece, Without Seams),
PAINTED ON BOTH SIDES WITH ARTISTIC DESIGNS, SUITABLE FOR ANY SOCIETY,

ALSO THE ACTUAL MANUFACTURER OF
Artistic and Durable Regalia of every description
FOR ALL SOCIETIES.

- -

Books, Summonses, Cards, Envelopes, Note Paper, Ballot Boxes, Iron Safes,
And every requisite necessary for properly conducting the business of
a Society or Institution.

- -

GOODS SENT BY RETURN MAIL TO ALL PARTS OF THE WORLD.

EXTREME CLIMATES HAVE NO EFFECT ON GEORGE TUTILL'S BANNERS.		GOODS CAREFULLY PACKED IN TIN-LINED CASES AND INSURED TO DESTINATION.

GEORGE TUTILL has supplied Flags, Banners, and Regalia for India,
Australia, New Zealand, West Indies, Canada, United States, Newfoundland,
The Orkneys, Gibraltar, and the most extreme points of the civilized world.

George Tutill advertisement, 1895.

Reputed to be George Tutill enjoying a private joke. This engraving appeared in his 1895 catalogue and shows him wearing the regalia sash of a Grand Templar – or do the initials stand for George Tutill, who kept his own silver tankard at the Star public house in City Road?

George Tutill's own cricket team on an outing to Wormley. The wicketkeeper, front row, seated second from left, is Charles Caffyn. The man in the centre wearing the bowler is H.W.E. Storey, who married Tutill's only daughter, Georgina.

Herbert Sharpe, one of the most talented of Tutill's centre painters, at work in 1935 on a replacement for the badly-torn banner of the Chopwell lodge (see page 107). Sharpe has 'squared up' the old banner for copying purposes. The oil paintings of religious scenes hanging on the wall are reputed to be the work of Tutill himself.

A general view of the ground-floor studio at City Road. Six banners are in the process of being painted, the silk stretched taut on wooden frames. The banner on the left is for a Methodist Sunday school, while that on the right is for a trade union.

Rose Thackray, an unidentified centre painter, Jack Pooley (a cornerman and signwriter), and Herbert Sharpe, at work on trade union banners in 1935. The banner in the foreground was probably for one of the dockside unions. The others are for the National Union of Boot and Shoe Operatives, Durham Miners' Association and the Amalgamated Engineering Union.

Trimming banners by hand in the upper gallery of Tutill's studios in the 1890s. The banner in the foreground is that of the Amalgamated Union of Operative Bakers and Confectioners, Staffordshire district.

A banner artist had to be versatile, working on a trade union banner one day and a Sunday school banner the next. Here a centre painter is completing a religious scene for a Sunday school banner, while in the background an unfinished banner for the Durham miners awaits completion.

The front cover of George Tutill's catalogue for 1905.

One of the brass name discs used to secure lead tapes to Tutill's banners made after 1861.

Tutill's standard letter of insurance for a new banner, dated 1914, requesting an annual premium of 1s. 6d. (7½p).

The Kenning copy of Tutill's original brass banner tag. The Kenning tag would not have been made until the 1880s.

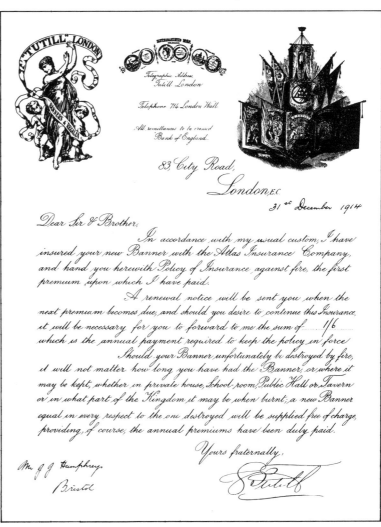

The largest Jacquard loom in the world, specially constructed and installed at Tutill's premises at 83 City Road, London, for the weaving of his patent banners. The punch cards which programmed the machine can be clearly seen in the foreground. The loom could weave an ornate pattern repeating every nine feet.

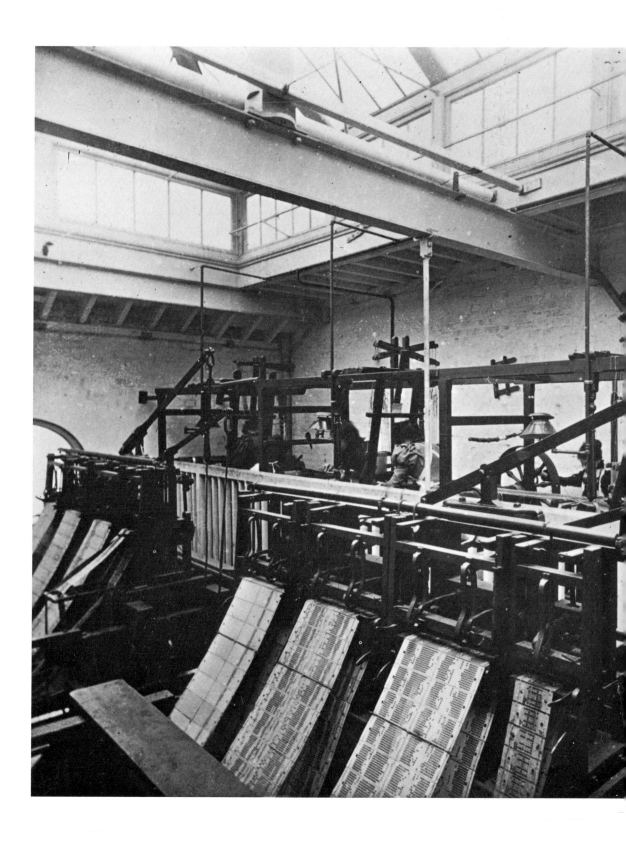

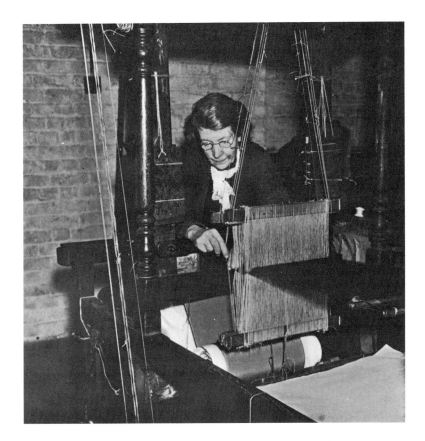

Miss Chitty, who worked for many years at Tutill's, weaving twelve-inch (30.5 cm) banner bordering. There were four of these looms in use at Tutill's until 1940.

Picking off small imperfections from the silk during the weaving of a silk banner on a draw loom.

The demonstration of trade unions to greet five members of the Alliance Cabinet Makers' Association on their release from Coldbath Fields prison in June 1875. They had been sentenced at the Central Criminal Court for the peaceful picketing of Jackson and Graham, a firm of cabinetmakers who had sacked their workers when they struck against the arbitrary introduction of piecework. Public opinion was aroused and a long trade union campaign eventually forced modification of the law. The released men were greeted by a crowd of 5,000 and drawn on a banner-decorated wagon to the Paul's Head tavern in Old Street, for a reunion breakfast with their families. Later in the day they were given a public dinner at the Cooperative Hall in Castle Street, attended by 400 delegates from many unions. Afterwards, the unions marched with banners and bands to the Reformers' Tree in Hyde Park for a meeting attended by more than 25,000. The leading banner could be that of the United Society of Coachmakers. The following two banners of the Cabinet Makers are obviously their national banners, but the one behind appears to have been made for the occasion, with the slogans 'Injured but not dead' and, rather ominously, 'We bide our time'.

COMBINED TO PROTECT

This banner of the United Tin Plate Workers' Society is the oldest authenticated trade union banner yet to be found. It was discovered in the Liverpool offices of the National Union of Sheet Metal Workers, Coppersmiths and Heating Domestic Engineers. The tinplate workers changed their name to sheetmetal workers around 1890 when new materials were coming into more general use in the old tinsmiths' trade. The receipt for the banner had also been preserved in the old Liverpool Society's box; it reads, 'To William Dixon for painting and washing etc. a Colour £0.5s. 0d.' and is dated 21 July 1821. The United Tin Plate Workers' Society was a federal body comprising a number of local societies, formed in 1821 and probably dissolved in 1825. Other local societies would have had similar banners as evidenced by a fragment of an old banner bearing the title United Tin Plate Workers' Society and showing a scrap of the coat of arms, found in the Glasgow office of the present union. The banner provides an interesting link with the medieval craft guild since the design is taken directly from the

armorial bearings of the Worshipful Company of Tin Plate Workers, alias Wireworkers. The local signpainter did not understand the guild blazon, hence the spherical ship's lantern, or 'rolling lamp', has become a globe of the world. The seventeenth-century oil lamps have also suffered from his interpretation. The supporters in their billycock hats, knee breeches and stockings are a down-to-earth rendering of seventeenth-century craftsmen instead of the richly attired supporters to be seen on the guild arms. The motto, 'Unite in love', is a direct translation from the guild's Latin motto.

This Tin Plate Workers' Society banner was also found in the Liverpool offices of the National Union of Sheet Metal Workers and is almost certainly the one referred to in the 1838 cash book of the Liverpool Society for 27 June of that year. The entries read, 'Sundrie bills for the colours 13s. 6d.' and 'Officers allowance, Looking after Colours 1s. 6d.' The 'Officers allowance' was probably for beer consumed when collecting the banner, the Liverpool Society frequently paying members in beer for such tasks. Union records show that a new banner had been ordered for the procession to mark the coronation of Queen Victoria and this would seem to be the banner in question. It depicts a number of symbols commonly used by early trade unions and friendly societies, the 'all-seeing eye' taken from the iconography of the Freemasons, the old Roman symbol of unity, the fasces, a bundle of sticks bound together and the allegorical figures of Hope and Justice. The whole design is similar to the emblematical design used on the membership card of the London Plate Workers' Society as early as 1805 when they were carried from local society to local society by trade union tramps seeking work.

The Friendly Society of Sawyers, Whitehaven, was one of a number of small sawyers' trade unions based at seaports during the nineteenth century. In 1816 it is recorded that the shipsawyers of Liverpool, a society of some 200-250 members, struck for higher wages. The men, although supported by other members of the trade from towns not on strike, were beaten after twenty-two weeks and forced to accept lower wages until 1823 when they struck again. This time the employers introduced blackleg labour and there was much violence, one man being killed and one of the yards set on fire. The Whitehaven sawyers must also have had their share of trouble, for most of the yards in Whitehaven were owned by the Lowther family who were fiercely anti-union.

The Whitehaven banner was carried in the 1838 coronation procession, when, according to the *Cumberland Packet*, some sixty sawyers took part in the march. The sawyers acknowledged allegiance on the obverse of their banner with the motto, 'Success to Victoria', but added a plea for 'Civil and Religious Liberty and Free Trade throughout the World'. The face of the banner recognises the close link of the sawyers with the shipbuilders, hence the prominence of the sailing ship. Also illustrated are the two types of saw in use at the time for cutting timber into planks and a small picture of a sawyer at work over a pit. The 'top-

sawyer' was a skilled labourer, but the 'pitman' who worked with aching arms above his head and with sawdust filled eyes was a manual labourer of the humblest order. The two supporters on the banner hold tools of the trade, a plumb line and carpenter's rule.

A bannerette rather than a banner, this emblem of the Friendly Association of Cotton Spinners measures 50.8 x 71.1 cm and is printed appropriately on cotton. The union was formed in 1806

and it is known that the banner was carried by Robert Tait, a cotton spinner, in a Reform demonstration in 1832. The photograph is taken from a japanned tin tray as the banner is too faded for reasonable reproduction. The image on the banner is similar, although it has the addition of the clasped hands of unity and the motto 'United to support'. The Glasgow Cotton Spinners were temporarily suppressed when five of their leaders were prosecuted in a case which like

that of the Tolpuddle Martyrs became a *cause célèbre*. Following a series of strikes, they were accused and charged with murder, arson and conspiracy. The jury unanimously rejected nine of the twelve charges brought against them but by a majority of one, found the men guilty of conspiracy to keep up wages and assaults at two factories. Sentenced to seven years' transportation, they spent three years in the prison hulks before they were pardoned in 1840. The banner is part of the People's Palace, Glasgow, collection.

Tursdale colliery opened in 1859 and the tattered lodge banner of the Durham Miners' Association is believed to have been made shortly after, probably in the 1860s. The banner is made of two layers of silk and the front of the banner curiously displays the emblem of the Friendly Society of Ironfounders which was designed by Chant and Saddler in 1857. The mystery is unexplained. Did the miners acquire the banner from a defunct branch of the Ironfounders and overpaint their own title and add their own second side? Or did they, taking a fancy to the industrial symbolism of the emblem, merely persuade the unknown banner painter to repeat the image for Tursdale? Whatever the answer, the lettered side with its curious figures is uncompromising for an early Victorian banner with its motto 'Unity, Combination and Liberty'.

Virtually nothing is known of this faded banner of the Edinburgh United Tobacconists. The Tobacco Workers' Union was formed in 1834 as the Friendly Society of Operative Tobacconists by a small group of journeyman tobacco spinners meeting at Jacob's Well, London, a popular meeting place for working class radicals. Various unions of United Tobacconists were formed outside London and it is assumed that the Edinburgh banner was made *c*.1835-1845. The banner carries the handshake of unity, the insignia of Scotland and England and familiar symbols of the industry, the supporters resting on a hogshead of tobacco with pouch and pipe in their hands. The banner is part of the Huntly House Museum collection, Edinburgh.

The Hull Seamen's and Marine Firemen's Amalgamated Association banner is a superb piece of marine painting by an anonymous artist. Painted in 1887 when the union was formed from a fusion of the Hull Marine Firemen's Mutual Association and the Hull Sailors' Mutual Association, the scenes include the perils of life at sea, the sailor's return home, the unity of sailors of both sail and steam, a lighthouse and the symbolic figure of Britannia. The steamship on the obverse flies the flag of 'Brotherly Love', while the motto on the face insists, 'God helps those who help themselves.' The Association amalgamated with the National Sailors' and Firemen's Union in 1922 and the banner was donated to the Hull City Museum by an old sailor who had preserved it in his home for many years. Measuring 3.05 x 3.05 m, it is one of the largest seamen's banners in existence. A larger marine banner was that of the Green's Home branch, of the National Amalgamated Sailors' and Firemen's Union, hardly portable at 4.88 x 3.66 m, but that banner, painted in 1895, does not seem to have survived.

A Scottish trade union banner carried in the great Reform demonstrations of 1832. The supporters depicting 'justice' stand beside a vast wooden sideboard carrying the masonic symbol of square and compasses. The banner, size 2.30 x 1.35 m, painted on white linen must have been made prior to the Reform demonstrations, for the 'reform' claim has been overpainted. While the motto is conciliatory, another banner of the Edinburgh Cabinet and Chairmakers proclaims, 'Let tyrants tremble while justice holds the scales.' Both banners are part of the Huntly House Museum collection, Edinburgh.

The Bristol District No. 1 Branch of the National Union of Gasworkers and General Labourers' banner is made up of two layers of silk and may actually be two banners made into one. The face of the banner, too faded to reproduce, is signed 'H.E. Stacey, Bristol 1893'. This is Henry Edward Stacey, a local watercolour artist and a member of the Royal West of England Academy. His banner painting illustrates scenes of a gasworks, pipe laying and work in a retort house. The back of the banner, illustrated, is smaller in size and sewn onto a larger panel to match the face. It is signed 'L. Stacey, Bristol, after Walter Crane'. The border of oak leaves, heroic worker figures wearing red caps of liberty and the angelic woman heading the design have all the imagery of a Crane painting. No record of L. Stacey, follower of Crane's art, has

been found but it is reasonable to assume he was a contemporary relative of Henry Edward Stacey. There is a popular claim in Bristol that the gas workers' banner was the first trade union banner to be carried through the streets of the city. To which side of the banner the story relates is uncertain but may well refer to the smaller banner in the style of Crane with its general motto, 'The cause of labour is the hope of the world', and could pre-date the 1893 banner to which it is joined.

The Preston branch of the Typographical Association was formed in 1849, and became the Preston branch of the National Graphical Association when the TA amalgamated with the London Typographical Society in 1963. Since 1882 the banner has been carried in the Preston Guild

Festival, an event that has been celebrated at twenty-year intervals since the sixteenth century. The guild account of the trades procession of 1882 describes the banner as 'new', though this could mean made since the previous festival of 1862. There is an item in an old account book of the association, dated June 1883, for the expenditure of 13s. 1½d. for the repair of banner boxes (there was a second, smaller banner, now lost), which may mean that the banner was already some years old by 1883. The face of the banner depicts Caxton examining the first proof. The obverse illustrates the motto '*Lux e tenebris*' – 'Light out of darkness'. The Latin tag '*Ars artium servatrix*' – 'Art which is the servant of the arts' – forms the base on which is seated Knowledge and the messenger.

The Society of Grain Millers was formed in Glasgow in 1884. Their banner was made by George Kenning, who had opened a Glasgow office about that time. The firm of Kenning had become George Kenning & Son before the turn of the century, so it is reasonable to assume that the banner was made shortly after the union's formation in 1884. The design is unusual for the period and has a graphic quality ahead of its time. In 1917 the Grain Millers were absorbed into the Workers' Union who in turn amalgamated with the Transport and General Workers' Union in 1922. The banner is now part of the National Museum of Labour History collection.

The Cleveland district banner of the Associated Iron and Steel Workers of Great Britain was unfurled on 30 May 1897. The national anthem was played by the Cleveland Steelworks silver band as the ceremony was performed by a representative of the employers, Mrs David Evans, wife of the manager of Bolckow Vaughan (the largest steelworks in Europe at that time). The portraits are of Edward Trow (top left), general secretary of the union, and John Kane (top right), the puddler who founded the original union, the Amalgamated Malleable Ironworkers' Association, in 1862. The scene depicts a meeting of the Northern Conciliation Board headed by Sir David Dale, and includes William Aucott, president of the union, James Cox, assistant general secretary, and Councillor E. Thomas. Last carried in a procession in 1905, the banner was lost until 1950 when it was discovered in the attic of The King's Head at Grangetown. It is now kept at the Middlesbrough office of the Iron and Steel Trades Confederation.

Vic Feather, late general secretary of the TUC, appears amused at the thought of workers going cap-in-hand to a smooth suited and spatted boss. The banner of the Manchester No. 13 branch of the National Union of Railwaymen must surely be the most obsequious trade union banner of them all. The motto 'Come let us reason together' is again biblical, Isaiah 1:18, and used on a number of early banners but seldom accompanied by such a humiliating illustration. The banner, discovered at the Star and Garter public house in Manchester in 1973, probably belonged originally to the Amalgamated Society of Railway Servants and was overpainted with the NUR title in 1913 at the time of the big amalgamation. Manufactured by the Manchester firm of H. Whaite, the banner has gone astray again in recent years and its present whereabouts is unknown.

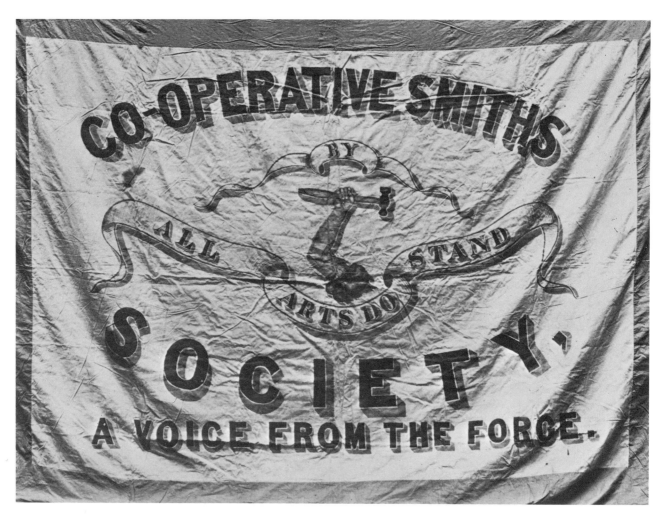

The Co-operative Smiths' Society was a small union of blacksmiths covering the area around Newcastle-upon-Tyne, formed in the 1870s. The banner, which dates from that period, uses the traditional 'uplifted hand', the proper sign of the blacksmith. The motto is an abridged version of the motto of the Worshipful Company of Blacksmiths: 'By hammer and hand all arts do stand'. After a series of amalgamations the society became part of the Amalgamated Society of Boilermakers, Shipwrights, Blacksmiths and Structural Workers. The banner is now kept at the Nottingham office of the General, Municipal, Boilermakers & Allied Trades Union.

Fred Hollingsworth, late president of the Amalgamated Union of Foundry Workers, remembered seeing this banner when he first joined the union at the beginning of this century. He said that the banner was old even then. The first Foundry Workers' Union was formed on 6 February 1809 at a Bolton-Le-Moors public house, appropriately called The Hand and Banner. The union was known as the Friendly Iron Moulders' Society and did not change 'Moulders' to 'Founders' until 1854. The emblem of the union on which the design is based was made in 1857 and it is possible that the banner may be of similar age. It belonged to the Sheffield and District branches, and is now part of the National Museum of Labour History collection. A similar banner of the Blackburn branch of the union can be seen at the County Hall of Blackburn Museum and Art Gallery.

It was not until 1872 that the hated 'yearly bond' was finally abolished. Bound to the colliery owner by the year, a miner could be hunted like a criminal if he left his work. Forced to put his mark to the iniquitous bond, he had to report for work every day of the year except Sundays; failure to do so usually meant summary conviction and imprisonment and Durham Gaol was seldom without its 'bond' victims. The owner had no obligation to provide work and if trade was slack he could send the men home without pay. He had the power to impose fines and could cheat the men without redress. In one case, a hewer sent eight trucks to the surface in his day's work. The checker, who was paid by the number of trucks he rejected as underweight, said seven of the eight were short. The miner was thus paid for one truck only, while the owner sold all the coal that the miner had hewn. To complain at such tyranny would mean not only the sack but eviction from his miserable cottage. The banner of the Monkwearmouth lodge of the Durham Miners' Association records the historic scene, when W.P. Roberts, popularly known as the 'Pitmen's Attorney General', successfully defended four miners charged under the Master and Servants Act and had their bond rescinded, giving the men the legal right to withdraw their labour without punishment.

1 Corinthians 13:11 supplies the motto for the North Stafford Miners' Federation banner of the Burslem No. 1 lodge. The scene illustrates the faith of Abraham, who is about to sacrifice his son Isaac. The ram in the thicket is just discernible. It certainly required faith to be a trade unionist in 1893, when the Burslem banner was made. Miners were taken to court and fined if they stayed away from work without sufficient reason. Hours were long, wages low and organised protest was met with lock-outs, victimisation and evictions. The North Stafford Miners' Union was formed in 1869; the date when the title changed to 'Federation' is not known for certain. The secretary of the Stafford Miners was Enoch Edwards, who later became president of the Miners' Federation of Great Britain in 1904. There are fine portraits of him on the Hanley and Longton branch banners, both of which are in the collection of the Chatterley Whitfield Mining Museum.

The Chatham district banner of the Amalgamated Society of Woodworkers is based on an earlier design for a certificate of membership for the Amalgamated Society of Carpenters and Joiners. In 1866 the executive committee commissioned a well-known artist of the time, A.J. Waudby, to design both an emblem and a certificate. Fortunately the artist's explanation of the original drawing is recorded. On one side of the banner (it is difficult to differentiate front and back when both are such fine paintings) is depicted Joseph of Nazareth, 'the most distinguished member of the craft on record, being the reputed father of our Saviour'. Justice bearing the sword and the balance and Truth holding a mirror are placed either side of him. The motto is 'Credo sed caveo' – 'I believe but I beware'. The obverse shows an illustration representing 'the centring of an arch adapted from a plate in Nicholson's practical carpentry flanked with a carpenter and joiner'. Both figures are based on a portrait of James Blayne, chairman of the executive committee in 1862 and branch secretary of the Camden Town branch in 1866. Blayne stated in 1896, when applying for superannuation, that the saw shown in the hand of the carpenter on the left of the design was still in his possession. The banner, according to an old member of the union, G.A. Matthews, was made about 1899; a 5s. levy was imposed on all members in the area to meet the cost. Mr Matthews recalls the banner being carried during local disputes and strikes before the First World War. Some time after 1927 the banner was returned to Tutill's for reconditioning and alteration to the name and title. It was last carried through the streets of the Medway town on May Day, 1962. The banner is now part of the National Museum of Labour History collection.

This fine banner, painted in George Tutill's studio, was found by strikers when they demonstrated at the offices of their own union, the National Union of General and Municipal Workers, during the Pilkington dispute at St Helens in 1970. The box in which the banner was found was lined with newspapers dated 1923 which may indicate the last time the banner was used. The Sheet Glass Flatteners were in existence in 1891 and the banner would seem to date from the last decade of the nineteenth century. The obverse of the banner illustrates the trade unionists' popular fable about the power of unity: 'A small child can break a single stick, but bound together a strong man cannot break them.'

The banner of the Belfast branch of the Amalgamated Society of Tailors illustrates the first people ever to wear clothes. This device has been used by tailoring trade unions for well over a century and seems to derive from the guild arms of the Worshipful Company of Needlemakers, whose first recorded use of the Adam and Eve figures dates from 1680.

The Amalgamated Society of Tailors joined with the London Society of Tailors and Tailoresses in 1932 to form the National Union of Tailors and Garment Workers. The reverse side of the banner carries the insignia of the city of Belfast and in 1973 the union presented the banner to the Ulster Museum, Belfast.

The banner design of the United Kingdom Society of Coachmakers is based on the guild arms of the Worshipful Company of Coachmakers and Harnessmakers. The union altered the arms by adding the royal standard and their own motto '*Surgit post nubila Phoebus*'. The reverse of the banner has yet another motto, 'In things essential, unity'. The banner carriage was invented and built in 1902 by the secretary of the Leicester branch, James Nicholson, who later became general secretary of the union. The strips at the top of the banner were added upon the amalgamation of a number of local coachmakers' trade unions in 1919.

The 1888 banner of the Operative Bricklayers' Society, Watford, is almost identical in design to a surviving banner of the OBS, London Order banner of the Leicester branch and the banner of the Norwich branch of the Amalgamated Union of Building Trade Workers. The bricklayers' union, originally known as the Friendly Society of the Operative Bricklayers, split into two sections, the London Order and the Manchester Order, in 1848.

The Watford banner design is a replica of the union emblem drawn by A.J. Waudby in the 1860s. The annual report of the Operative Bricklayers' Society for 1869 details expenditure of £115. 0s. 0d. to Waudby for the painting of a 'new flag'. In view of the huge cost for the period, it could be that Waudby himself painted the first bricklayers' banner to carry his emblematical design. The complex design depicts the first bricklayers building the Tower of Babel and includes a reminder that 'Every house is builded by some man, but He that built all things is God'. The intricate design, said by Waudby to 'not merely serve the purpose of a trade emblem, but to form an elaborate and interesting work of art', includes the allegorical figures of Truth and Prudence, the three sisters of Architecture, Sculpture and Painting and the emblems of peace and industry – the dove and the beehive. Euclid and Sir Christopher Wren feature in the design as do an operative bricklayer in his working clothes and a foreman with a plan in his hand. An unusual feature of the magnificent Watford banner is the very beautiful pole tops, silver trowels in place of the familiar brass-coloured spearheads. They were presented to the society by the well-known company of W.H.S. Hunt & Sons, Brades, in 1888. The initials of W.H.S. were commonly said by the brickies to stand for 'Work hard and starve'. The banner is now part of the National Museum of Labour History collection.

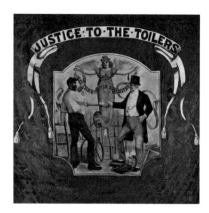

'Dockers' Union' was commonly used as an abbreviation for the Dock, Wharf, Riverside and General Labourers' Union which arose out of the Great Dock Strike of 1889, taking in the Tea Operatives' and General Labourers' Union of 1887, with the revolutionary engineering worker Tom Mann as president and Ben Tillett of the Tea Operatives as general secretary. It is therefore likely that the Ipswich Dockers' Union was a branch of the national organisation and not merely a local union. There is no record of when the banner was made, but the ship in sail appears as a standard design in George Tutill's catalogue of 1896 and so it is probable that it was painted around that date. The motto on the obverse, 'Justice to the toilers', would seem to conflict with the painting of a top-hatted employer with cash box and moneybag at his feet. Certainly, the plea for unity between the workers and the boss was in conflict with the militant policy of the union's leadership at that time.

The original banner of the Tea Operatives' and General Labourers' Association, formed by the tea operatives of the Cutler Street warehouse, led by Ben Tillett. This banner was used throughout the Great Dock Strike of 1889 for the 'dockers' tanner' and for some years after. Ben Tillett wrote of 'our old dockers' banner, a linen sheet on which was thickly painted in black the name of our organization. It meant mud and road refuse as a bouquet, only too often.' Later, this banner was sewn on to a silk banner bearing a portrait of Tillett and inscribed to commemorate the historic struggle.

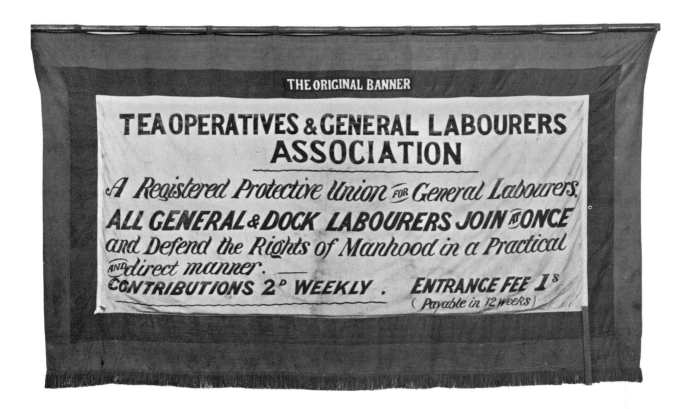

Perhaps the best of the banners commemorating the solidarity of the Australian wharfies with the British dockers during the Great Dock Strike of 1889 when Australian workers collected and sent more than £25,000 to the starving dockers. The banner, 3.66 m high, was painted in oils by an artist of Tutill's onto one of the famous embroidered silk backgrounds woven on the great Jacquard loom, probably just after the conclusion of the strike. A similar design with slight variation, the figure of Britannia being replaced with the figure of Unity for example, was made for the number five branch of the union and it is likely that other branches also made use of the image. In the 1920s, the Plaistow and the Barking branches of the Dock, Wharf, Riverside and General Workers' Union used the same design, changing Britannia and Unity for a female figure of Liberty with a 'bonnet rouge'.

The first London May Day demonstration led by trade unions, 4 May 1890. The banner of the Woolwich Arsenal engineers depicts an 'eight hours shot being fired in the direction of Parliament'.

In 1898, at an Electrical Trades Union Delegate Conference at Manchester, the Loughborough branch proposed that a banner should be purchased. A design was commissioned from Walter Crane, the socialist painter and illustrator. The ETU could not have made a better choice, for Crane, a friend of William Morris, was a talented artist who gave of his best for the cause of Labour. Although Crane designed the banner, it is doubtful whether he actually painted either of the two identical banners that survive. They would probably have been executed by a professional banner painter from Crane's original artwork. Crane's 'angel of freedom' first conceived by him for a painting, *Freedom*, exhibited at the Grosvenor gallery in 1885, provided the inspiration for the design of countless other trade union banners.

Discovered in 1967 in the basement of Kingsley Hall, Bristol, this magnificent banner of the National Amalgamated Society of Operative House and Ship Painters and Decorators is now in the Bristol City Museum collection. In 1968, during the TUC centenary celebrations, a competition was organised to find the best banner in the city. The painters' banner was successful and it was presented to the city by George Woodcock, general secretary of the TUC at that time.

In October 1983, during the refurbishing of the Jubilee Hall at Burton, Stoke-on-Trent, workmen removed a panel below the stage to discover this long-forgotten banner of the Burton-on-Trent Society of Painters and Decorators. The union amalgamated with the National Amalgamated Society of House and Ship Painters in 1904 and the banner, with its motto 'Defence not Defiance', would seem to date from the late nineteenth century. Painted onto a surfaced calico, the banner carries no maker's name or signature and would seem to be the work of a member of the branch. The home-made box in which the banner was kept would support this view. The coat of arms with Latin motto '*Honor alit artes*' ('Honour fosters the arts') are those of Burton-on-Trent.

The tools of the trade, the paperhanger's scissors, paste brush and paperhanging brush on one side and the artist's palette with mahlstick and signwriter's brushes on the other, represent the decorating and decorative aspects of the trade. Through the consideration of the site foreman, R.N. Fell, and the enthusiasm of H. Byrd, the Burton-on-Trent secretary, the banner was eventually delivered to the regional office of UCATT. Ken Barlow, the regional secretary, arranged for the cleaning and restoration of the banner by Chippenham Designs, which regretfully included some extensive re-painting. The banner was hung on display in the Regional Office on the 7 November 1984, where it remains.

WIDOWS AND ORPHANS

A rare photograph of a docker's
funeral in Custom House, East
London. The banner, led by union
officials wearing their sashes, would
head the march to the local cemetery.
The picture was taken in 1928.

Railway workers and their families with an old banner of the Paddington branch assemble in Hyde Park for the TUC organised protest against the Industrial Relations Bill on 21 February 1971. The illustration is another variation on the 'dependent family' scene and carries the biblical quotation so popular with the pioneers of trade unionism: 'Bear ye one another's burdens.'

Details of the corner paintings of the banner of the Operative Bricklayers' Society emphasize the hazards of the trade and the security offered by membership of the union. Benefits for accident, sickness, old age and death were of vital importance in an age when social security was unknown. The incapacity of the family breadwinner could quickly mean the shame of 'going on the parish' or even to the workhouse.

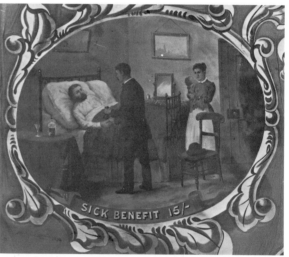

'The last good morning', a Victorian picture story, was painted on the Monkwearmouth banner of the Durham Miners' Association in 1921. The design originates from the 1870s and has been updated only by the style of dress. The theme may well have been used to adorn the Monkwearmouth banner carried at the first Durham Miners' Gala in 1872. In the right-hand section of the cameo, a trade union official is seen representing the widow and orphan at a claim for compensation.

Although this graveside scene with its Elizabeth Barrett Browning quotation at the head has all the appearance of a Victorian tragedy, it was in fact painted for the Stockton branch of the National Union of Railwaymen in 1914. The design was almost certainly copied from an earlier banner of the branch when it would have been part of the Amalgamated Society of Railway Servants, formed in 1872. In 1879 the executive committee sent a letter to all branches suggesting that an orphan fund should be set up under the control of the union and at the AGM that year passed a resolution that 'each member should contribute one halfpenny a week to the Orphan Fund'. The banner painting includes a likeness of Help, the faithful collie presented by a Mr Riddell as a travelling collector on behalf of the Fund in 1882. Help raised over £1,000 for the railway orphans by the time of his retirement in 1889 and upon death was stuffed and placed on Brighton Station where he continued to raise 12s. to 15s. a week for the Fund. The bereaved family are watched over by the 'all-seeing eye of providence' and are assured of funeral and death benefits from the union. The banner is now in the collection of the Dorman Museum, Middlesbrough.

Harry Gosling, first president of the
Transport and General Workers'
Union, lying in state in a banner-
draped hall at Transport House,
October 1930. The banner behind the
coffin is that of the Greenwich branch
of the Amalgamated Society of
Watermen and Lightermen. Born on 9
June 1861, Gosling was the son,
grandson and great-grandson of
Thames watermen, and himself
became a freeman of the Watermen's
Company. He joined the Watermen's
Union in 1889 and became general
secretary of the Society in 1893 at a
salary of £100 a year. He was elected
president of the National Transport
and General Workers' Union in 1922.

The corner paintings from this early banner of the National Union of Vehicle Workers may be lacking in artistic skill, but they give a complete story of concern and help offered by the union to a member in need. The first scene shows an accident caused by a faulty wheel. Next, union officials, complete with regalia sashes, visit the injured man in hospital. The third scene shows the officials calling on his family and offering sympathy, and the last shows the successful union claim for compensation.

THE ACCIDENT

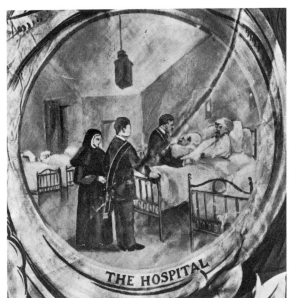

THE HOSPITAL

SYMPATHY

VERDICT FOR PLAINTIFF

An English cottage with flowers around the door, a cat, loving wife and a pipe present a composite, cosy picture of retirement for a member of the Amalgamated Society of Toolmakers. The union, formed in Birmingham in 1882, offered membership to blacksmiths, fitters, engineers, turners, borers, planers, shapers, drillers, slotters, general toolmakers, bicycle, tricycle and sewing machine makers. This small craft union whose motto was 'It is by helping others we best help ourselves', concentrated on funeral, accident and superannnuation benefits as the advantages of union membership. The retirement scene depicted on the union banner is taken from part of the union's emblem, designed and printed by Percival Jones Ltd of Birmingham. The photograph of the banner was found in an old Tutill sample book and it is not known if the banner has survived.

An important activity for any trade union in an industry as hazardous as mining is to represent members who have contracted disease or suffered injury as a result of their work. This banner of the Durham Miners' Association shows the union official watching as the injured member receives the doctor's or specialist's report. The union would then ensure that the medical report was acted upon and fight for fair compensation.

One of the many unions catering for building labourers in the 1920s was the National Builders' Labourers' and Constructional Workers' Society which stemmed from the United Builders' Labourers' Union founded in November 1889. Obviously they saw friendly benefits as a powerful incentive to recruitment. These two banners of the Surbiton and Camberwell branches of the union, made in 1921, feature the £100 disablement payment and the promise of union support in the case of industrial injury. The union eventually amalgamated in 1952 with the craft union, the Amalgamated Union of Building Trade Workers, which in turn became part of the amalgamation that formed the Union of Construction, Allied Trades and Technicians in 1971.

The spirit of brotherly help is illustrated on the eighty-year-old banner of the North Stafford Miners' Federation. The scripture, from Galatians 6:2, 'Bear ye one another's burdens' is used to convey the promise of mutual help provided by the union in times of injury, sickness and death. The composite painting on the face of the banner again shows a biblical influence – the lamb lying with the lion and angels administering to the sick and bereaved. The banner was made by George Tutill.

A perfect illustration of the appeal of a 'coffin club' trade union. Among early societies the friendly aspect of the union's activities were all-important and funds were unlikely to be dissipated on strike pay. The United Society of Boiler Scalers and Stoke Hold Labourers was formed in 1902 and the banner dates from the founding of the union. It is now part of the National Museum of Labour History collection.

A familiar danger for the drivers of horse-drawn transport, the loss of a wheel and consequent injury. The obverse of the banner shows the concern of the union officials for their brother worker, visiting him wearing their sashes of office. The picture carries the scripture from Matthew 25:36: 'I was sick and ye visited me.' The vignette, top left, shows the payment of death benefit to the widow, while the illustration opposite depicts the widow at the graveside. The reference beneath the title, 'Late 61 L.C.T.U.' refers to the London Carmen's Trade Union which became part of the National Union of Vehicle Workers in 1891. The banner which must have been made shortly after the amalgamation is now in the collection of the National Museum of Labour History.

Formed in 1911, the United Order of General Labourers of London was one of the expansive unions ready to recruit labourers in the London Docks, weakening the unity of dockworkers that had grown from the 1889 strike. The banner illustrates the importance the union placed on death and accident benefits with its picture of a union official handing cash to a widow. Note the union emblem, framed and hanging on the wall of the living room scene. The obverse of the banner is headed 'accident' and shows the official bringing cash to a member with his arm in a sling. An unusual feature of the banner is the words incorporated boldly within the design on the obverse, 'This banner is the property of the members of No. 6 branch'. The banner is now part of the National Museum of Labour History collection.

HEROES

◄ The Heworth banner was made in 1947, partly to replace the old banner which was in bad condition, but also to mark the Act of Parliament passed on 12 July 1946 by the 1945 Labour government nationalising the mining industry. The obverse of the banner depicts Manny Shinwell, the Minister of Fuel and Power, handing a copy of the Act to Lord Hyndley, the first chairman of the National Coal Board on Vesting day, 1 January 1947. The face of the banner carries a fine portrait of Keir Hardie, 'the apostle of British socialism', honoured on more trade union banners than any other man. Hardie, born in poverty in 1856, first worked in a mine at the age of ten as a trapper and was elected as the first labour member of Parliament in 1892. Heworth colliery closed on 17 June 1963 and the banner was cared for until 1973 by a veteran of forty-five Galas, former Heworth lodge secretary, Joe Hall. He said, 'It's a great banner, but nationalisation or not, we always had Keir Hardie on the front.' The banner is now kept at Beamish, North of England Open Air Museum.

Voices from the past are echoed by the portraits of three pioneers of mining trade unionism, Tommy Ramsey, Alexander McDonald and William Crawford. Ramsey died in 1873, McDonald in 1881 and Crawford in 1890. Haswell colliery closed in 1895 so it is likely that the banner was carried in not more than four or five galas which would account for the fine state of preservation of such an old banner. Ramsey, or 'old Tommy' as he was known to the men, was a hero of the 1844 strike and a founding member of the Durham Miners' Association. A rough and ungrammatical speaker he was gifted with the warmth of expression that communicated directly with his class. His portrait shows him wearing his top hat and carrying the famous crake and handkerchief that he used for rallying miners to his meetings. Better known is Alexander McDonald, 'the miners' friend', who started work in the mines at the age of eight. Victimised for his part in the 1842 strike against intolerable conditions in the Lanarkshire coalfield he fought his way to a university education and became general secretary of the Scottish Miners' Union. He was elected as an early representative of the miners to Parliament, winning Stafford as a Liberal candidate in 1874. William Crawford was chosen as the first general secretary of the Durham Miners' Association in 1869, having previously been secretary of the Northumberland Miners' Association. A conciliator with a dominating personality he was a skilful negotiator and commanded the respect of the miners and their employers alike. It was Crawford who chaired the first 'Big Meeting' in 1871 and like McDonald he became a Liberal MP representing the miners.

The obverse of the banner depicts four more mining trade union pioneers, William Patterson, John Forman, John Wilson and John Johnson. The banner is now part of the collection at Beamish, North of England Open Air Museum.

The banner of the Bilston Glen branch of the National Union of Mineworkers carries two portraits, both of militant miners' leaders: A.J. Cook and Abe Moffat. Moffat came from a family of miners and was born in the important pit village of Lumphinnans, in the heart of the Fife coalfield, on 24 September 1896. He left school at fourteen and followed his father down the mines. He was elected justiceman (checkweighman) in 1928, an important position for defending the interest of the miners. Moffat knew long periods of unemployment and blacklisting for his militant activities on the miners' behalf. He served as general secretary to the revolutionary United Mineworkers of Scotland for a time and in later life became president of the National Union of Scottish Mineworkers. His portrait remains on a number of Scottish banners as a tribute to his work.

A.J. Cook was a champion of Britain's miners. Born in 1885 he left school to work in the pits of South Wales for twenty-one years. A lay preacher in his early life, he never lost his revivalist style of oratory. Even after winning the elections as secretary of the Miners' Federation of Great Britain in 1924, he still toured the coalfields at weekends agitating. Men would walk for miles to listen to Cook and soon a greater trust was put in him than had ever been given to a miners' leader. R. Page Arnot, the official historian for the miners, wrote

There has never been a miners' leader like Arthur James Cook; never one so hated by the Government, so obnoxious to the mine owners, so much a thorn in the flesh of General Secretaries of Unions, never once in his three years' mission from 1924 to 1926 has so much unfeigned reverence and enthusiastic report been given from his fellow miners.

It was Cook who led the miners in the General Strike of 1926 and who continued to lead them in their lone fight when the strike was called off. In every mining village there is someone who will speak of Cook, even to this day. The banner of Bilston Glen is a witness to the memory of a man who never betrayed the trust the miners put in him. The Bilston Glen banner was originally made for Roslyn colliery, and when the pit was closed it was taken to the miners' welfare. Unable to display it to advantage, they let the banner go to Bilston who had the name altered. Cook must have been honoured on scores of miners' banners but the caption beneath his portrait on that of the East Hetton lodge of the old Durham Miners' Association seems to epitomize the thoughts of those who remember him. It reads, 'Faithful unto death'.

Wardley was one of the mining villages known in the 1920s as 'Little Moscow'. The banner of Follonsby lodge made about 1924 can leave little doubt that the title was appropriate. Inspired by the revolution of the Russian workers, the miners at a full General Meeting of Follonsby lodge voted their revolutionary heroes on to the lodge banner: Lenin, father of the first socialist state, James Connolly, socialist hero of the famous Easter Rising, A.J. Cook, the militant miners' leader, Keir Hardie, the legendary British socialist, and George Harvey, a local miner known popularly as Wardley's Lenin. The banner is evidence of the intensity of the struggle between the coalowners and the miners in the two decades before the Second World War. Unhappily, the banner has not survived. The socialist heroes were

picked off one by one over a period of political and social change. Lenin, Connolly and Harvey had all been painted off the banner by 1947, and replaced by three union officials, A. Joyce, T. Smith, and another local official, E.C. Justice. Only photographs survive as a reminder of the revolutionary socialist commitment of the Wardley lodge. By good fortune, the glass negative from which this print was taken escaped the bombing of Tutill's in 1940. Follonsby colliery closed in 1969 and the new banner is now kept by the Wardley British Legion.

Chopwell was another of the 'Little Moscow' villages. First painted by Tutill's in the early 1920s, the banner was badly torn during a demonstration and another banner, exactly the same, was ordered in 1935.

The idea of putting portraits of Marx and Lenin along with Keir Hardie on the Chopwell banner is attributed to some of the left-wing members of the lodge, including Harry Bolton and the Lawthers, Eddy, Steve and Will (later Sir William). The lodge decided to

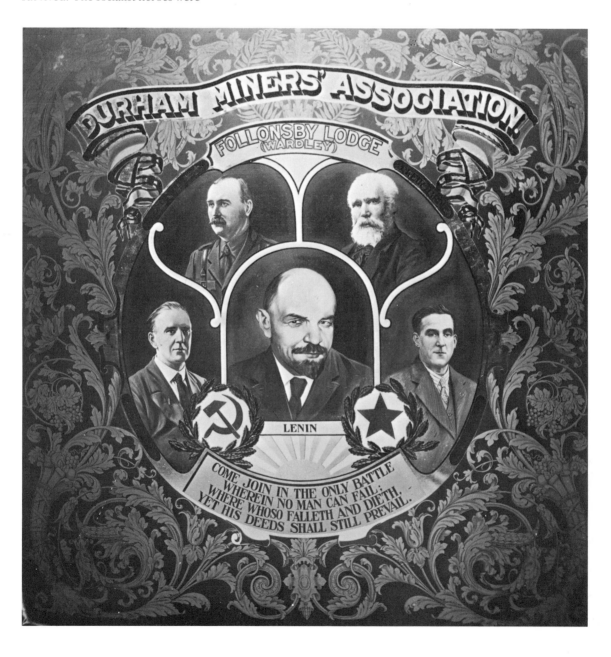

send Steve Lawther to Ireland to bring Jim Larkin, the founder of the Citizen Army and militant general secretary of the Irish Transport and General Workers' Union, to Chopwell to inaugurate the banner. The banner was unfurled outside the Chopwell Working Men's Club on a Friday evening prior to the Gala. The verse on the banner, 'Pioneers, oh pioneers', is from a poem by the great American, Walt Whitman. In 1954 a delegation of Russian miners from the Donbas visited the Durham coalfield and were invited to call on Chopwell lodge. It was at this time that Chopwell had purchased yet another replica of the original banner, and the old banner was presented to the Russian miners as a gift from the miners of Chopwell. It was said that the banner would hang in the Hall of Trade Unions in Moscow, a fitting resting place for the relic of the militant British miners who earned for their village the name of 'Little Moscow'.

Designed by executive council member John Hepplewhite for the 125th anniversary of the founding of the union. Each of the twenty-two districts of the United Society of Boilermakers, Shipbuilders and Structural Workers has a banner of identical design. Made by the Birmingham Regalia Company of Fattorini, the banners carry illustrations of the products of the labours of the union members and a portrait of a former general secretary, Ted Hill. The massive Cockney leader of the boilermakers was born in West Ham in 1889 and was apprenticed in the ship repair yards on the Thames. He joined the boilermakers in 1916 and was active as a shop steward after serving in the First World War as a marine. He became general secretary of the boilermakers in 1948 and was a member of the TUC General Council from 1948 to 1965. Ted Hill surprised and dismayed many old comrades when he accepted a life peerage in 1967. The boilermakers' union amalgamated with the General and Municipal Workers' Union in 1982.

The Elemore lodge of the Durham Miners' Association chose two pioneers of Labour from North and South for place of honour on their banner made by Tutill in 1924. Peter Lee was born in 1864 in the colliery village of Trimdon Grange and started work in the colliery at ten years of age as a pony driver. By sixteen he was working at the coal face and in 1887 was delegate from his lodge to the Durham Miners' Council. He became general secretary of the DMA in 1930 and became president of the Miners' Federation of Great Britain in 1933. Lee had a long record of service as a local and county councillor and the new town of Peterlee is named after him. Lansbury was born in 1859. A Christian pacifist, he was lifelong champion of the poor of London's East End and lived among them for seventy years, even when he became a Cabinet Minister. First Labour mayor of Poplar, founder of the *Daily Herald*, leader of the Labour Party, imprisoned for his activities on behalf of the unemployed and the cause of women's suffrage, Lansbury was the conscience of the British Labour movement of a half a century. He was guest speaker at the Durham Miners' Gala on seven occasions between 1912 and 1938.

The Northern Ireland Area of the Amalgamated Society of Painters and Decorators' banner honours Robert Tressell, author of *The Ragged Trousered Philanthropists*, the novel that became the bible of the building trades. The name under which his classic account of working class life was published is a pseudonym, for he was Robert Noonan, born in obscure circumstances, probably in Dublin in 1870, and buried in a pauper's grave in Liverpool on 10 February 1911. The banner, by an unknown painter, is believed to have been made in the 1930s and was presented to the Ulster Museum, Belfast, by the Union of Construction, Allied Trades and Technicians in 1979. Noonan, a decorator and signwriter by trade, is said to have painted a number of banners for the labour movement, but the only one positively identified, and possibly the only one surviving, has not been seen since 1940. Painted for the Hastings branch of the Social Democratic Federation in 1910, the banner depicts a shirt sleeved worker wrestling with the writhing serpent of capitalism, an image derived from Walter Crane. The SDF title on the banner was altered in 1929 to that of the Independent Labour Party and was last known to have been carried in public in the great May Day march in London in 1937. The banner was removed from Hastings to Birmingham for safekeeping during the invasion threat in 1940 and its present whereabouts, like Noonan's early life, remains a mystery waiting to be solved.

◀ Painted in 1947, the banner of the Dean and Chapter lodge of the National Union of Mineworkers pays tribute to many famous names, Dalton, Lawson, Shinwell and Ellen Wilkinson among them. Place of honour is given to a local hero, Billy Todd, whose portrait is in the centre of the banner. Todd was a local Communist miner who was victimised by the coalowners in the 1930s for his activities on behalf of miners. He was eventually re-employed at Dean and Chapter colliery in 1941, on the intervention of Ernie Bevin, at that time Minister of Labour. Billy Todd became secretary of the lodge later that year, was elected to the Durham Area Executive in 1942 and finally to the executive committee of the NUM in 1944. He died the following year at the age of forty-five.

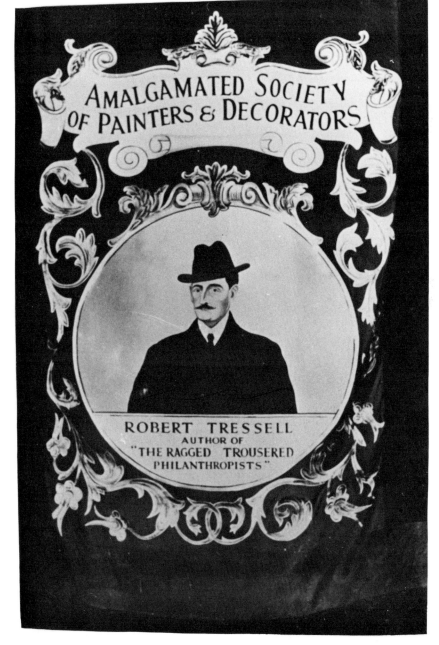

The idolatry of men is an uncertain affair; not all heroes of labour are 'faithful unto death'. The Tursdale lodge banner of the Durham Miners' Association is a reminder of betrayal. On this banner the legendary Keir Hardie is flanked by two lesser mortals bathing in reflected glory. They are the Rt Hon J. Ramsay MacDonald and the Rt Hon Philip Snowden. That they were heroes at the time they were honoured by Tursdale there is no doubt. MacDonald in particular was an idol of the labour movement and featured on miners' banners throughout the country. The exact date of the painting of the banner is uncertain, though it is likely to have been 1924. The fact that both portraits are captioned with 'Rt. Hon.' as titles indicates that both were in government office when the banner was painted. Snowden, who was first elected to Parliament in 1906, held his seat until 1918 but lost it in the election of that year because of his pacifism. MacDonald too opposed the war and lost his seat. Snowden regained his place in the Commons in 1922 and became Chancellor of the Exchequer in 1924 in the first Labour government. MacDonald had to wait until 1923 to be returned as member for Aberavon. Snowden opposed the General Strike of 1926, which was called in support of the locked-out miners who, already living in poverty, were resisting a wage cut and an increase in hours. As Chancellor of the Exchequer in the 1929 Labour government headed by MacDonald he proposed a 20 per cent cut in unemployment benefits and the introduction of the means test as part of his scheme to solve the economic crisis. When MacDonald deserted the Labour government in 1930, Snowden joined him as Chancellor in the National government.

The banner of Bewicke Main lodge portrays MacDonald in even stranger company, surrounded by four militants, including Lenin. The lesser known of the five portraits is that of Ben Oliver, a checkweighman who was chairman of the lodge. Oliver was also chairman of the Labour group of the Chester-le-Street Rural District Council in the 1920s, and it was in that capacity that he fell foul of the Conservative government during the 1926 strike. Throughout the long struggle he arranged for the Public Assistance Board to sit every week to examine the cases of destitute miners and such was the sympathy and support of the Council that it was surcharged and its members suspended.

When MacDonald betrayed the Labour movement in 1930, the miners in fury removed his portrait from their banners. Some were carried during the 1931 Gala with holes cut in them where MacDonald's portrait had been, while others were painted out or otherwise mutilated. When the Bewicke Main banner was discovered in a neglected state in Birtley during the late 1960s, it was found to show the portraits of Keir Hardie, Lenin, Ben Oliver and A.J. Cook with a large white circle of paint in the centre. When the painted circle was washed away, the portrait of MacDonald was revealed, as fresh as the day it was painted. Alderman E. Cowan, a former chairman of Bewicke Main rescued the banner, and as the lodge had been closed since 1947, presented it to the Oliver family who displayed it in a club house in Bewicke Main. The banner is at present on loan to the Kibblesworth Junior Mixed Infants School where it hangs as a reminder of the loyalty of four men to the cause of socialism and the betrayal of that cause by the renegade, MacDonald.

The National Amalgamated Sailors' and Firemen's Union was founded by J. Havelock Wilson in 1887 and went into voluntary liquidation in 1894. This massive banner (3.66 x 2.44 m) would have been made during that period. The figure of the sailor beneath the motto, 'Divided we fall', bears a strong resemblance to Wilson himself. In his autobiography, Wilson commented on this practice:

> Then again, everyone's portrait had to be painted on the banners. The national men (that is to say, the leaders of national importance) had first place, such men as John Burns, Tom Mann, Ben Tillett, Will Thorne and myself. I think my record would compare favourably with many of the national leaders in the way of appearing on banners; this was largely due to the fact that I was described as a stormy petrel and my activities brought me more in touch with the poeple who had the banner craze. I've seen at the Durham miners' demonstrations my portrait painted on as many as fifty banners, and of course as far as the Seamen's Union was concerned no banner could be complete without my painting in all kinds of picturesque positions. I have sometimes appeared very much like a parson, at least from the appearance of the painting I might well have been taken for a clergyman. At other times I would appear in a more picturesque role, such as that 'heroic sailor' Jack Crawford, the hero of the naval battle of Camperdown, where a sailor was depicted hanging on to the stump of a mast nailing the Union Jack to it.

A pioneer of trade unionism among dock workers was Ernest Bevin, honoured on the Bristol Carters' branch banner of the Dockers' Union. As a young man, Bevin worked as a carter in Bristol in 1901 and led the carters into the Dock, Wharf, Riverside and General Workers' Union in 1910, making Bristol a stronghold for the union. For a decade, Bevin campaigned for unity and the amalgamation of a group of transport unions to form the Transport and General Workers' Union, to which he was elected as the first general secretary in 1922.

The banner bearing Bevin's likeness also carries the British and Australian coats of arms, recalling the unity of British and Australian dockers during the 1889 strike. The photograph is taken from an old Tutill sample book and it is not known if the banner is extant.

It is fitting that the Warwickshire County banner of the National Union of Agricultural Workers should bear the portrait of Joseph Arch, the farm labourer and lay preacher who organised the isolated farm workers into their first national trade union in 1872. Arch, who began his working life as a bird scarer at the age of nine, was born in the south Warwickshire village of Barford in 1826. The present banner was purchased by the County Committee in 1948 from George Tutill at a cost of £100, the money being subscribed by many of the district branches and the balance raised by a draw. The idea for the banner was mooted in the early 1940s and it was planned to unfurl it beneath the branches of the famous chestnut tree at Wellesbourne, where Arch held his first meeting of farm labourers on 7 February 1872.

Unfortunately, the tree died in 1948, shortly before the banner was ready. However, the banner was unfurled on the site and dedicated by the vicar of Wellesbourne with full choir in attendance. Union members marched to the ceremony headed by the Chipping Campden Band, taking the same road from Barford to Wellesbourne that Arch walked on that historic day, seventy-six years earlier.

A tribute from London watermen and lightermen to the role of Cardinal Manning as mediator in the Great Dock Strike of 1889. Unlike his counterpart, the Archbishop of London Dr Temple, who answered Ben Tillett's appeal with 'a letter full of the most virulent abuse of the docker and his claim for a higher wage', Manning endorsed the dockers' main claim for 6*d*. per hour. The reverse side of the banner bears the guild arms of the Worshipful Company of Lightermen, complete with the motto 'At commande of our superiors'. It also carries the date 1514, in reference to the first Act of Parliament to regulate fares upon the Thames, and also 1559, the date of the re-incorporation of the guild.

Admiral Bedford Clapperton Trevelyan Pim, RN, was born in 1826 and was Conservative MP for Gravesend, 1874-80. His presence on the Greenwich branch banner of the Amalgamated Society of Watermen, Lightermen and Bargemen is something of a mystery. The reverse side of the banner, which bears the guild arms of the Worshipful Company of Watermen, has a river scene showing the newly built Tower Bridge, with sailing ships and lightermen at their work. Tower Bridge was not completed until 1895, which means that the decision to honour Pim by the union was not taken until after his death in 1886. As an MP for Gravesend, Pim would have represented the watermen in his constituency and it is possible that he spoke in defence of their ancient river rights at some time during his short parliamentary career, as did Colonel C.E. Hamilton, whose portrait was painted on the banner of the Bermondsey No. 3 branch in September 1890. Whatever the reason, the banner is unique and Pim remains the only Admiral to grace a trade union banner.

Heroes all! Women's support groups on the march with the miners during the great strike of 1984-5. The lead banner is from Easington lodge, Durham, and bears the portraits of former general secretary of the National Union of Mineworkers, Lawrence Daly, and pioneer of mining trade unionism, Tommy Hepburn. The third banner, also from Durham, has portraits of another three great champions of mining unionism, A.J. Cook, Keir Hardie and Aneurin Bevan.

The Bentley branch banner of the National Union of Mineworkers is only one of a number of banners bearing a portrait of the union's president, Arthur Scargill. The banner was made in 1980 by Chippenham Designs of Norwich, but the centre portrait was painted by Margaret Burlton, an artist well known for her paintings of mining life and work. A successful portrait painter, Burlton's work reached a turning point when she visited Betteshanger colliery in the Kent coalfield in 1974. She became obsessed with the idea of capturing underground work in her paintings and obtained special permission from the National Coal Board to sketch miners below ground in Kent and South Wales. Her resulting paintings have been exhibited at the Royal Academy and Gallery Poll in West Berlin. Though non-political herself, Margaret Burlton says she was 'moved by the comradeship she found in the pits' and 'grew to admire the movement for its honest struggle to gain a better deal for its members'.

The decision to make the banner and to pay tribute to Arthur Scargill was taken at a special branch meeting and the members contributed a 10p weekly levy to pay a total of £1,800 for the completed banner. The motto, 'The workers united will never be defeated', was proposed by the branch secretary, 'Jock' Nimmo, a former Lanarkshire miner with more than forty years service as an underground worker. The obverse of the banner depicts the memorial in Arksey cemetery to forty-five miners killed at Bentley in 1931 and to a further seven who perished at the pit in 1978.

A WORLD TO WIN

To raise the money to buy the Southall branch banner of the Associated Society of Locomotive Engineers and Firemen in the 1920, engine drivers would pick up boxes of fish from Grimsby in the early hours of the morning and bring them on the footplate to London for sale. The reward for months of fish sales and fund raising was the superb banner painted by George Kenning & Son. The militancy of the men in this period is perfectly captured by the illustration conceived by the Southall members, showing a trade unionist breaking down the barriers of capitalism and trampling 'secret reports' and private ledgers underfoot. The portraits are of Albert E. Fox, general secretary 1901-14 (left) and John Bromley, general secretary at the time the banner was made. The banner featured prominently during the fight against the 'Beeching Cuts' and is still carried on demonstrations to this day.

The influence of the syndicalists is clearly seen on this banner of the Rickmansworth branch of the National Union of Railwaymen. Syndicalism, or industrial unionism, held that all production and therefore all society depended on the industrial workers. They simply had to refuse to produce for profit by 'folding their arms' to bring the downfall of capitalism. The forming of the NUR from the three separate societies of the Amalgamated Society of Railway Servants, the General Railway Workers' Union and the United Pointsmen and Signalmen's Society was welcomed by the syndicalists, who sought to build unity and strength by welding the trade unions into a dozen or so unions, each based on a whole industry, instead of the 1,800 separate societies that there were before 1914. The Rickmansworth banner captures the mood of the syndicalists with the class-war slogan and demand for industrial action to free the workers from the chains of capitalism, but also expresses the policy of the non-syndicalist members of the branch who saw the ballot box as their road to the cooperative commonwealth.

The Mantle and Costume branch banner of the National Union of Tailors and Garment Workers proclaims the aim of the union – to build a socialist commonwealth. The design of the banner is copied from an earlier banner of the United Ladies' Tailors' and Mantle Makers' Union, originated by Jacob Fine when he was general secretary in 1918. The union amalgamated with the National Union of Tailors and Garment Workers in 1939 and the banner was painted about that time at a cost of £93. The obverse of the banner carries the motto of the old United Ladies' Tailors' Union, 'Toiling tailors true together'. It was found in 1969 in the basement of the Charles Square office of the union in London.

The banner of the National Federation of Women Workers was unfurled in March 1914. Made by the firm of Toye, the design is taken from the Walter Crane illustration for the cover of the union's weekly journal, *The Woman Worker*. The badge depicts Unity, illustrated by the bundle of sticks bound together, and the familiar handshake, so long the symbol of trade union unity. The object of the union is clearly stated on the banner, 'to fight, to struggle, to right the wrong'. Appropriately, the first president of the union in 1906 was the indefatigable fighter for better pay and conditions for women, Mary Macarthur. At the unfurling of the banner it was declared that it was 'to be used at all industrial disputes where women are involved', In November 1918, at the end of the war, some 5,000 women who had been sacked from Woolwich Arsenal marched to the embankment where the Federation banner was held aloft while Mary Macarthur addressed the crowd. Wherever the fight involved women, Mary Macarthur and the Federation were there, helping to organise Dundee jute workers, Bridport networkers, Kidderminster carpet girls, and dozens of other groups. The leaders of the Federation believed passionately in equality for women and as soon as a male-dominated union was prepared to open its ranks, the Federation transferred whole branches to the men's union. Finally, in 1920, the Federation amalgamated with the National Union of General Workers.

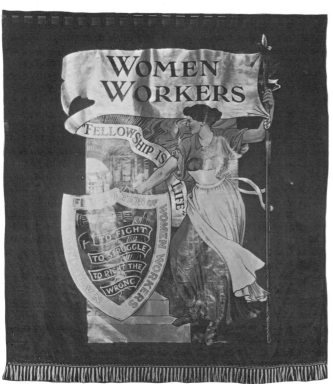

◀ The death of a pit. The mourners wear black armbands for the last march of the Wombwell branch banner at the Yorkshire Miners' Gala in 1969. The banner carries black draping to mark the closure of the colliery after 113 years. Leading the march is their branch secretary, Roy Hepworth, who lost his leg in a mining accident. After a century of struggle to end the poverty and oppression familiar to every miner before nationalisation, the banner records the achievements and the goal. Wombwell could not have foreseen the last step before socialism as the sack.

This must be one of the most class-conscious and uncompromising trade union banners ever made. The fight to organise labour has never been easy, especially among unskilled and semi-skilled workers. During the hard times after the First World War, when this banner was painted, there were many attempts at strike breaking by the employers. The trade unionist on the left of the banner tells the boss to 'stand back', while his brother unionist deals with the blackleg illustrated on the right.

Trade union banners in Hyde Park, 1922, to support the unemployed in their demand for 'work or maintenance'.

A poignant reminder of the misery of sweated labour among Jewish workers in London's East End. The banner is said to have been designed by Israel David Goldman (Tubby Goldman), the general secretary of the union, in 1924, the year the union was founded. Though not the work of a professional banner painter, the banner movingly portrays the plight of women machinists who were worked till exhaustion. The Yiddish phraseology of the banner offers hope and a poor tailoring worker points to the rising sun of socialism with its promise of a better life for all. The London Trousers Makers' Union became part of the National Union of Tailors and Garment Workers in 1936.

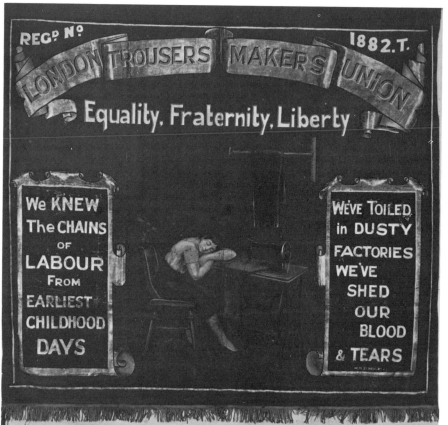

This banner of the Bermondsey branch of the National Union of Public Employees was purchased in 1932 at a cost of £33. Up until 1939 the banner was always carried on May Day, which was a public holiday for council employees in the Labour borough of Bermondsey. The banner was used in the 1946 campaign for a £5 minimum weekly wage, then lost when the member who had been responsible for its safekeeping died. Ten years later the banner was discovered in the Neckinger Depot at Bermondsey during reorganisation of the borough. It featured prominently during the 'dirty jobs' dispute of 1970 when the union fought for a 55s. increase for its members. Of the eight vignettes on the banner, two illustrations recall the past, the great council lock-out of 1921 and the hated means test of unemployed workers and their families.

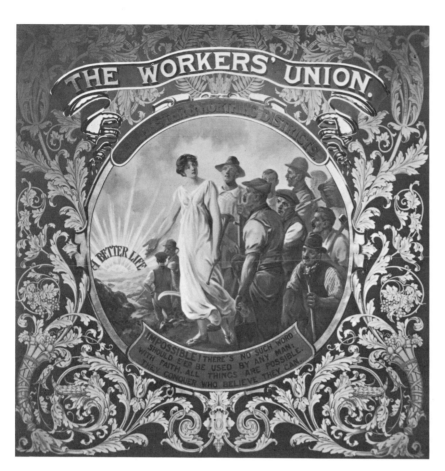

The dream of a better life is a recurring theme on trade union banners from earliest times. These banners of general workers' unions made shortly after the First World War reflect the socialist conviction of the leadership of unions organising labourers and unskilled and semi-skilled workers. Tom Mann, who helped found the Workers' Union on May Day, 1898, had been a prominent member of the marxist Social Democratic Federation and was to become a founder member of the Communist Party in 1920. Will Thorne, founder of the Gasworkers' Union in 1889, was also an early member of the SDF and had enlisted the help of Eleanor Marx in building the union where she was elected to the executive committee. When the Gasworkers' Union changed its name to the National Union of General Workers it was Marx's son-in-law, Edward Aveling, who drafted the objects of the union. The defeat of capitalism and the creation of the cooperative commonwealth was a theme repeated on scores of banners from the general workers' union.

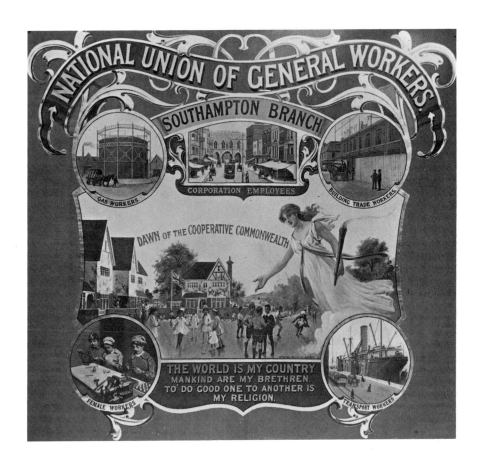

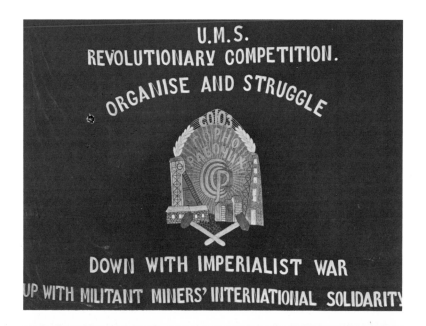

Made in the Soviet Union, this banner was presented to the United Mineworkers of Scotland by Soviet miners in 1931, when the Scottish Union was affiliated to the Red International of Labour Unions, the trade union arm of the Communist International. The UMW was formed in 1929 after a dispute about elections for the leadership of the Scottish Mineworkers' Union, when the old leaders refused to recognise the election results which the militants claimed they had won. When the officials refused to vacate their positions, the militants formed their own United Mineworkers which lasted until 1936. The banner was presented as an expression of solidarity between the miners of Scotland and the Soviet Union, which began with the illegal journey of two Scottish miners, James Stewart and David Proudfoot, to the Soviet Union in 1920 for a conference of revolutionary trade unions.

The banner is one of a number presented to mining trade unions by Soviet workers, an earlier example being the banner given by working women of Krasnoya Presna, Moscow, to British miners and their wives following the lock-out and General Strike of 1926. The banner was brought back to Mardy and kept in the Workingmen's Hall where it was used on special occasions, including the funerals of local communists when it was draped over the coffins.

The militancy of the 'new unionism' is vividly portrayed by a Herculean worker wrestling with the 'serpent of capitalism'. The design derives from Walter Crane's illustration of 'Hercules and the Old Man of the Sea', drawn for *A Wonder Book*, published in 1892. Tutill's, who made the banner, frequently used Crane's work as a ready reference for trade union banner designs. The banner would have been painted in the early 1890s and the forceful slogans represent a break with the conciliatory mottoes of the old craft unions. The reference to prostitution on the banner reflects the policy of the union which was formed during the Great Dock Strike of 1889 and aimed to change the wretched social conditions that prevailed in London's dockland at the end of the last century. A recent discovery of some old glass negatives that escaped the bombing of George Tutill's in 1940 show that the design was later copied, including the mottoes, for the New Monkton Main branch banner of the Yorkshire Mineworkers' Association.

To be present at any South Wales Miners' Gala Day is to be left in no doubt as to the commitment of the miners' union to the cause of socialism. Banner after banner proclaims, 'The future is ours – through socialism'. The banner of Risca lodge is a reminder of the enthusiasm with which British miners acclaimed the nationalisation of the mines by the 1945 Labour government. The Jefferson quotation on the Tower lodge banner has acquired a new significance with the run down of the coal industry. Of the colliery banners shown, only the Tower lodge and Morlais lodge pits remain open.

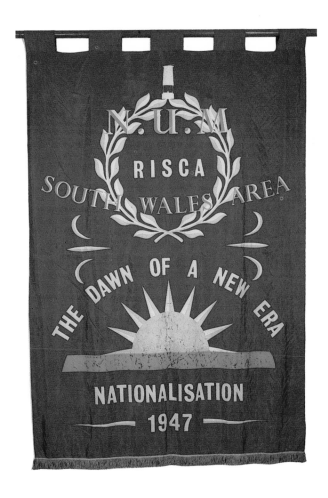

Detail from a banner of the National Union of General and Municipal Workers.

This banner of the Transport and General Workers' Union depicting a docker pleading with the establishment is probably older than the title would suggest. Such a picture of servility does not accord with the position of the TGWU which was formed in 1922 and the banner may have belonged to an earlier dockside union and over-painted with the new name at the time of the amalgamation.

Formed at the Horse and Sacks in the Edgware Road, London, after the First World War, the Shamrock branch was given its name by the large number of Irish building workers employed in the area at that time. The design of the banner is a Tutill copy of the front cover of the 1894 Christmas edition of the *Labour Leader* drawn by Walter Crane. The few lines of poetry at the bottom of the banner are also by Crane, being taken from the last verse of a Christmas poem written by him for the same issue of the paper. The motto 'The cause of labour is the hope of the world' was a favourite of Crane's and accords with the socialist commitment of the branch. The other side of the banner is yet another Crane design, 'The International Solidarity of Labour', drawn by Crane in 1889, which depicts workers of all lands holding hands in unity around the globe with the slogan, 'Freedom, fraternity, equality'.

The pictorial parable has appeared in many forms on trade union banners since the 1840s and is completely Victorian with its moralising emphasis on self-improvement. The undated banner of Merrington lodge contrasts the lot of two fourteen-year olds, one rich, the other poor, and demands the right of secondary education for the children of the workers. The 1930s banner of the Yorkshire Miners' Association demonstrates the rewards of trade union membership, shown by the well-dressed and well-fed family. The dreadful alternative for the unorganised worker is poverty and starvation.

Solidarity! The dockers and banners out, Tower Hill, 1912. The banner on the left is that of the London Carmen's Trade Union, and would have been made in the 1880s. The other is a Rotherhithe branch banner of one of the dock unions.

Local trade unionists with their branch banner at Witney, just after the First World War. The organisation of the Workers' Union was developed in this area during the war, particularly at the famous Witney blanket mills. The obverse side of the banner is characteristic of the militant origins of the union showing one of the many popular versions of David (the worker) slaying Goliath (the giant, capitalism). The banner was in perfect condition when found in 1969, having been kept in the original wooden banner box for fifty years. It is now part of the National Museum of Labour History collection. Two other versions of Tutill's allegorical imagery survive but only as prints taken from a batch of glass negatives found in December 1985. The East Ham branch of the old Dockers' Union illustrates a curious figure, a Spartacus with the helmet of Mercury using the sword of 'combination' to destroy a centurion representing 'capital'. The later version of the Swanscombe Street branch of the Transport and General Workers' Union shows a heroic worker killing 'poverty' and 'capitalism' with his bare hands, before the very citadel of 'capital'. The rising sun of 'solidarity' brings the hope of decent council housing in place of slums and the promise of a better life for all.

The design of the Plymouth branch banner of the National Union of General and Municipal Workers is based on 'The Triumph of Labour', a cartoon by Walter Crane. Drawn by Crane to commemorate the first international labour May Day in 1891, it was dedicated to the 'wage workers of all countries' and proved to be a popular source of inspiration for banner designs, even until the 1930s. It is perhaps surprising to see the NUGMW proclaiming 'the land for the people', one of Crane's favourite socialist mottoes.

Designed by Ken Sprague and made by Mountain and Molehill in 1960, this ETU banner is hand sewn and made of a variety of man-made fibres. The clenched fist, the workers' salute, is cleverly stylised to portray the power of the electricians and is typical of the strength of Sprague's designs. The banner is now part of the National Museum of Labour History collection.

THE BANNER BEARERS

Members of the National Union of
Bookbinding and Paper Workers on
strike from the Mugiemoss Paper and
Board Mill Company in 1936.

A miners' gala day is always a family occasion. Here, children enjoy a free ride through the streets of Rotherham during the Yorkshire miners' demonstration in 1981. The smooth running carriage carries a modern replica of the old Treeton banner, made by Turtle and Pearce in 1980. The original banner, too frail to be carried, was made about seventy years ago and is still kept at the colliery.

The 1958 Gala of the Nottinghamshire miners saw an innovation in banner carrying, man-power giving way to horse-power. Blidworth colliery produced 'Titch', a twelve-year-old redundant pit pony, led by his owner Mr George Richmond, a former ostler at the Blidworth pit.

The 1938 Durham Miners' Gala. Banners in huge numbers are arranged behind the platform as the audience awaits speeches from Attlee, Lansbury and Dalton.

The making of the Northampton County banner of the National Union of Agricultural Workers was first proposed on 4 October 1947. The cost of the banner, £77 10s. 0d., was raised by holding a prize draw, tickets 6d. each. On 13 June 1948 the banner was carried in a procession headed by the Northampton Silver Prize Band to a dedication ceremony at All Saints' Church, Northampton. The new banner was taken into the church furled, and during the singing of the appropriate hymn, 'Fight the good fight', unfurled and borne up the aisle to the altar where it was offered to the Reverend Canon Trevor-Lewis. He dedicated the banner with these words, 'We ask you to dedicate this banner, that it may be to us for all time a sacred symbol of loyalty to God, our King, and country, and of our intent to play our part in hastening the day of God's Kingdom among our fellow-men in this, our island.' The banner was placed

upon the altar and dedicated by the vicar 'as a symbol of loyalty to God and our fellow-men, and as a witness to the people of our unity in seeking what is just, honourable, and true'.

Some 600 members were present for the ceremony, including the mayor of Northampton, Sir George Chester, member of the TUC General Council and Ron Warwick, county secretary of the union. After a celebration tea, the banner was carried to the market-place for its first appearance at a public meeting. Both the president and the general secretary of the union were among the speakers. Since then, the banner has been used on many demonstrations, including the annual Tolpuddle rally, and is displayed at annual conference and district dinners. The reverse side of the banner shows scenes from the old farm worker's daily life, including hedge-laying, milking and stacking corn.

The banner of Murton Miners' lodge is carried into Durham Cathedral for the annual Gala Day service. The tradition was started in 1897 at the instigation of the Brass Band Association, who invited the Durham miners to take part. John Wilson, the general secretary of the DMA, agreed, but obviously with some reservation as his monthly news circular of June 1897 indicates – 'There may be (as we know there are) those who differ from the Bishop on his theological views: but whatever opinions we hold on those matters, we are bound to admit that his Lordship is very liberal on his ideas on social questions . . .'

The Murton lodge banner paying tribute to the 'Loyalty and Endurance' of Aneurin Bevan was originally made for Handen Hold lodge which closed in 1968. The lodge name was overpainted and the banner first paraded by Murton in the 1972 Gala.

A demonstration of farm workers in Bedfordshire. The woman is Miss F. Saward, the organiser. The man in the centre of the back row in front of the banner is Harry White, the district organiser.

A demonstration at Letchworth in the 1920s of members of the Amalgamated Union of Building Trade Workers, Eastern Counties division. This division covered Norfolk, Suffolk, Essex, Bedford, Hertfordshire, Cambridgeshire, Huntingdonshire, Buckinghamshire and parts of Northamptonshire and Lincolnshire. The banner was badly torn during a demonstration in Hyde Park in support of unemployed workers during the 1930s and no longer exists.

The destruction of a banner, ripped to shreds by high winds during a 1933 demonstration of trade unionists against wage cuts and unemployment. ▼

◄ One of the earliest of the stevedores' banners. Poplar stevedores had formed their own organisation, even before the Labour Protection League was founded in November 1871. They affiliated to the League as branch No. 3 in 1872. The banner would have been made in the early 1880s. The picture was taken during the historic strike for 'the dockers' tanner' in 1889. Daily marches through the city with banners and bands played an important part in arousing public sympathy, raising funds and sustaining the morale of the hungry strikers.

The London Cabdrivers' Trade Union was formed in 1894, and this magnificent banner dates from that time. The vignette within the horseshoe on the top right of the banner depicts the driver of a hansom cab in dispute with two passengers. The picture is captioned 'persecution'. This is a reference to what the cabbies called 'double justice' where licensed cabdrivers were liable to prosecution in the court and then could be dealt with again by the Public Carriage Office for the same offence. The picture on the top left shows the union defending a member in court. The union changed its name in 1913 to the London and Provincial Union of Licensed Vehicle Workers. The picture would have been taken shortly before that time.

Miners carry their banners through the streets of Hanley, Stoke-on-Trent, during a demonstration of unemployed in the 1920s. The banner in the middle reads 'What shall a man do when the capitalist cannot employ him?'

The banner of the Liverpool branch of the National Union of Dock Labourers at a mass meeting of seamen and dockers during the 1911 transport workers' strike, when 70,000 dockers, seamen, carters, tramwaymen and railway workers were out in the city. Tom Mann, one of the leaders of the 1889 Great Dock Strike, was again one of the leaders of the Liverpool strike, a bitter struggle which almost amounted to civil war when warships were moored in the Mersey, their guns trained on the city. Troops were called in and two workers were shot.

Members of the Amalgamated Union
of Building Trade Workers, Reading,
with their branch banner, during the
1920s. The photograph was taken on a
Sunday morning and the branch
members are dressed in their Sunday
best. The banner was last carried
during the General Strike of 1926, and
has since been lost.

The executive committee of the
London United Trade Committee of
Carpenters and Joiners during the
strike of 1891. Doubtless, though
dressed up for their visit to the
photographer's studio, they reflect the
confidence and comparative wellbeing
of skilled craftsmen, enjoying a far
better life than the unskilled and, at
that time, largely unorganised
labourers.

Leather straps, brass buckles and pole
cup are clearly seen as two miners hold
aloft their banner at a 1930s gala. Eight
men would form a team to carry the
banner, two to each pole and one on
each guide rope and tapes. On a long
march, the men would change places
to give the bearers a rest from the
strenuous task.

From the earliest days of banner bearing, miners have draped the lodge banner with black to mark the death of a comrade killed at work. In June 1984 the banner of Kellingley colliery was edged with black and carried at half mast at the Yorkshire Miners' Gala in memory of Joe Green, a branch member killed by a lorry while on picket duty at Ferrybridge power station during the 1984-5 strike. As a mark of respect, the marching order was changed to allow the Kellingley banner to head the demonstration.

5 March 1985 and the miners of Maerdy colliery, the last pit in the Rhondda, return to work after the great strike. At 6.30 am on a frosty morning they marched back, united and proud after a year of bitter struggle in defence of their jobs and community. With banners flying, the colliery band playing, escorted by women's support groups, friends and neighbours and led by their mayor, Cllr. Mrs Rees, the miners went back as one in a final demonstration of unity. The Maerdy banner bears the motto, 'Peace – forward to socialism'.

The Bower Unit banner originally belonged to Garforth Trench colliery and is reputed to be over 100 years old. When Garforth Trench was closed because of flooding in 1929, the banner lay unused until 1945. It was then purchased by Primrose Hill colliery for £50, which was put into the miners' welfare fund. The banner was renovated by a Leeds firm and overpainted with the new title, at a cost of £20. The banner, seen here at a Yorkshire Miners' Gala in 1958, was originally made by Breens of York Road, Leeds.

Trade unionists are not only to be found in grim industrial towns amid machinery and smoke. At the village of Tolpuddle in Dorset each year trade unionists from the countryside together with their brothers from the towns meet to commemorate the six farm labourers from their village who were transported in chains for daring to form a trade union. With all the atmosphere of an English village fete, the banners are raised and carried to the local churchyard where one of the martyrs, James Hammett, is buried. Hammett, who was brought home after serving five years of his sentence, died in the workhouse in 1891. When they buried him in Tolpuddle churchyard the squire stood by the grave to make sure that no one spoke for or on behalf of trade unionism. The Dorset County banner of the National Union of Agricultural Workers bears the final words of a poem, written on a scrap of paper by George Loveless and tossed above the heads of his guards to the watching public as he was being taken away to captivity, 'We will, we will, we will be free'.

WORK

The unusual design of the banner of the National Winding and General Engineers' Society is another example of Tutill's fine work. Made in 1926, the scenes around the pit-head illustrate power in industry as related to the work of the members. The obverse of the banner carries a portrait of C.W. Allison wearing mayoral robes. Allison, a union officer, was mayor of Stockton-on-Tees for two years and a member of Stockton Council for fifty years. Established in 1859, the union amalgamated with the Transport and General Workers' Union in 1935.

There is a nostalgic glimpse of the early days of aviation in this banner of the National Union of General Workers. The union was formed in 1889 by Will Thorne, as the National Union of Gasworkers and General Labourers of Great Britain and Ireland, and joined with the National Amalgamated Union of Labour and the Municipal Employees' Association to form the National Union of General and Municipal Workers in 1924. The experience of national bargaining gained by the trade unions during the First World War gave a great impetus to the drive for amalgamation in all sections of industry. The slogans on the banner, calling for fewer unions,

together with the paintings of RAF planes from Hendon Aerodrome, would date the banner from the time of the First World War or immediately after. It is uncertain whether members of the union actually worked at the aerodrome. It is more likely that Hendon, synonymous with aviation in those days, provided a graphic and immediate identification of the geographical location of the branch. The obverse of the banners carries the motto 'Unity, fidelity, love', which was adopted at a meeting of 2,000 gas workers in Victoria Park on 20 May 1889 at a meeting chaired by Will Thorne.

Founded in 1868, the Cumberland Miners' Association was a comparatively small union, with most of its members in pits close to the ports of Whitehaven and Maryport. In 1895 the union membership was 4,700, which would suggest that the union could never have possessed many banners. The Association affiliated to the Miners' Federation of Great Britain when it was formed in 1888, and became part of the National Union of Mineworkers in 1945. This banner was made by George Tutill in the period just before the First World War and is an exceptionally fine example of a colliery scene.

◄The district banners of the Amalgamated Engineering Union were all made to a standard design in 1950. One side depicts the union badge, with the motto 'Educate, organise, control'. Tom Mann was general secretary of the Amalgamated Society of Engineers, prior to the amalgamation, and then of the newly formed AEU. Mann had been a member of the Social Democratic Federation whose membership card carried the words 'Educate, organise, agitate'. The old motto of the ASE was 'Defence not defiance', hardly the sort of clarion call to come from a militant like Mann. It seems likely that he was responsible for the new motto of the AEU, borrowing from the old SDF motto, which itself goes back at least to Owenism, and changing 'agitate' to 'control'. The work of the members is illustrated on the other side of the banners with a composite scene showing the products of engineering skill. These may vary slightly from district to district but are basically the same. The date of manufacture of the banner may be observed from the registration number of the lorry, in this case GT 1950, indicating that the banner was painted by George Tutill's in that year.

Made in 1960, 100 years after the forming of the Amalgamated Society of Carpenters and Joiners, the forerunner of the present Amalgamated Society of Woodworkers. The banner was made by Toye and the materials and workmanship are of the highest standard as expected from this ancient company. The figure paintings, however, are strangely crude and perhaps demonstrate that the art of the banner painter was beginning to die.

The Northampton banner of the Nos. 1 and 2 branches was purchased in the 1920s at a cost of £80. Although the National Union of Boot and Shoe Operatives was not formed until 1873, both the motto and St Crispin have much earlier associations with shoe-making trade unions. There is a record dated 1834 that Nantwich shoemakers 'engaged Mr Thomas Jones to paint for us a banner emblematical of our trade, with the motto "May the manufactures of the sons of St Crispin be trod upon by all the world", at a cost of twenty-five pounds'.

A banner similar to that of the Northampton branch was carried in a trade union demonstration in Belfast in 1893. 'The Orangemen took a notion of the long-bearded St Crispin and his likeness to their Arch Antipathy, whereupon shouts of "To hell with the Pope" and stones and bricks flew and as a result the banner bearers rolled up the banner and flew for their lives.'

The present banner, which was used on May Day parades in Northampton for many years, is now on permanent loan to the Northampton Art Gallery and Museum. There is another banner of the union, which carries a similar inscription, hanging in the Norwich office of the union. This was purchased in 1919. The oldest surviving banner of the union dates from 1907. It is stored at the Bristol office and has deteriorated to a poor condition.

Blackburn was one of the earliest and most important district associations in the Lancashire weaving industry; it was formed in June 1854. It was the Blackburn Association that took a leading part in the agitation for the abolition of steaming in weaving sheds – which was a practice injurious to health – and who gave valuable evidence on behalf of the workers at the Steaming Enquiry of 1888. In 1858 the Blackburn Association became part of the newly formed East Lancashire Amalgamated Power Loom Weavers' Friendly Association, in an effort to combat the employers who were themselves joining together to crush the weavers' unions of the smaller towns. Eventually, in 1884, twenty-nine district associations of weavers combined to form the present Amalgamated Weavers' Association. The banner is thought to date from the end of the nineteenth century and is kept in the County Borough of Blackburn Museum.

Banners depicting women at work are comparatively scarce and mainly confined to the textile trade unions. The banner of the Oldham and District Weavers', Winders', Reelers', Female Warpers' and Cord Cutters' Association shows a calico loom with a woman weaver at her work. The print is taken from George Tutill's catalogue of 1895 and the banner described as being eleven feet by ten feet (3.35 x 3.05 m) in size, made of blue silk, trimmed with an orange border with a blue and white fringe. The obverse of the banner showed members of the union at their tasks of winding, warping, cord cutting and reeling.

A home-made banner of the Coventry branch of the National Union of Vehicle Builders. Made in 1945, it is the product of a cooperative effort organised by Arther Ince, chief shop steward of the Standard Motor Company at that time. The spruce for the poles was supplied by the motor company and machined in their sawmill. A car-trimmer made the leather straps and sockets, and a coachpainter, George Plummer, painted the banner, based on the other NUVB banner designs. The significance of the Mosquito aircraft in the centre of the design is that it was built at Standard Motor Company during the Second World War. The Latin inscription reads 'The sun rises after the clouds'.

The banner of the Manchester and District Council of the National Union of Railwaymen is designed to show the unity of railway workers of all grades in the industry following the amalgamation of 1913. The initials of the old railway companies LNER and LMS are well known, but what of 'G.B.R.' painted on the cab? Are they the initials of the banner artist, an obscure local railway company, or a look to the future of Great British Rail? The tender carries the date, 1926, commemorating the solid support of the union for the miners during the great lock-out and General Strike. The obverse of the banner depicts the benefit scene of widow and orphans which so often featured on NUR banners.

This charming banner of the Kidderminster Carpet Weavers' Association was made in the 1940s, to replace the old banner of the union which had fallen to shreds. Unfortunately, the older banner no longer exists. The face of the banner includes two replicas of the union badge, which is comprised of a shuttle, an Axminster spool bobbin and a yard bobbin. The verse is taken from the old banner which used to depict a union official making payment of benefits.

To walk along a London street is no hardship for the 'spider-men' who can be seen balancing precariously on narrow girders high above the city streets, erecting the steel frames of modern buildings. Formed in 1924, the Constructional Engineering Union also included crane drivers and others engaged on the engineering side of the construction industry. The union became an autonomous part of the Amalgamated Union of Engineering Workers in 1970 and in 1984 became part of the Engineering Foundry and Construction Section of the Amalgamated Union of Engineering Workers.

Taken in 1954, the picture shows the late general secretary of the union, Frank Stanley (beneath centre of banner wearing hat), marching with union members on a wage-claim demonstration. The Liverpool branch of the union also possesses a fine banner of similar design.

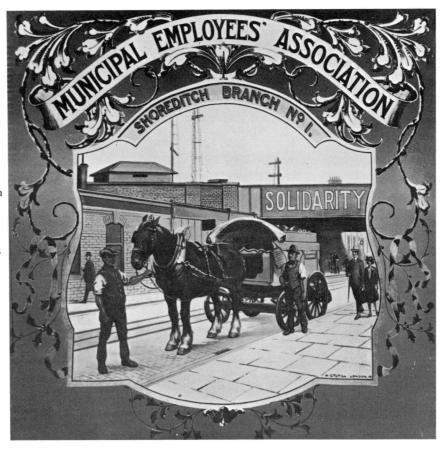

The Municipal Employees' Association was founded in 1894 and was part of the amalgamation which formed the National Union of General and Municipal Workers in 1924. Members of the MEA included road workers, dustmen, tramway workers and pier attendants. The union grew rapidly during the First World War and the Shoreditch banner would have been made about that time.

The name 'Altogether' was a vital part of the full title of the Builders' Labourers' and Constructional Workers' Society, formed in 1920 at a time when the labouring side of the building trade was split into many factions, including the Navvies' Union, the United Builders' Labourers' Union, the United Order of General Labourers and the National Association of Builders' Labourers. The 'Altogether' reflected the aim of the new organisation to unite builders' labourers in one union. Both these banners were made by Tutill's in 1921, when the union claimed a membership of 100,000. It became part of the Transport and General Workers' Union in 1934.

PLATE MAKER.

The Amalgamated Society of Holloware Pressers and Clay Potters, the China Potters' Federation and the Printers' and Transferers' Society amalgamated to form the National Amalgamated Society of Male and Female Pottery Workers in 1906. The banner of the National Amalgamated Society, which is now kept at Hanley Museum, dates from that time and was made at the banner shop of Henry Slingsby in Seymour Road, Nuneaton. The scenes of the banner show the differing tasks of the society's members. The holloware presser made holloware from moulds, as opposed to flatware, that is, cups and bowls as opposed to saucers and plates. The job of the placer was skilled as it required a knowledge of temperatures for the kiln. The motto, 'Our cause is just and firm will stand', at least seems to show a sense of humour on the part of the executive that approved the pun. The union became the Ceramic and Allied Trades Union in 1969.

PRINTER.

PLACER.

PACKER.

Railway enthusiasts for the age of steam will no doubt find significance in the position of the signals and be able to identify the railway company from the working of the signalman in the top picture. This banner of the Hornsey branch of the National Union of Railwaymen was made by Toye just after the amalgamation of 1913. The design emphasises the unity of all grades and the illustration of the locomotive is indicative of the pride of the railway worker for his industry. The National Railway Museum, which does exhibit some employers' banners, would surely benefit if the workers who operated the railway industry were represented by the permanent loan of a few trade union banners from stations and branches which are defunct. The banner is now part of the National Museum of Labour History collection.

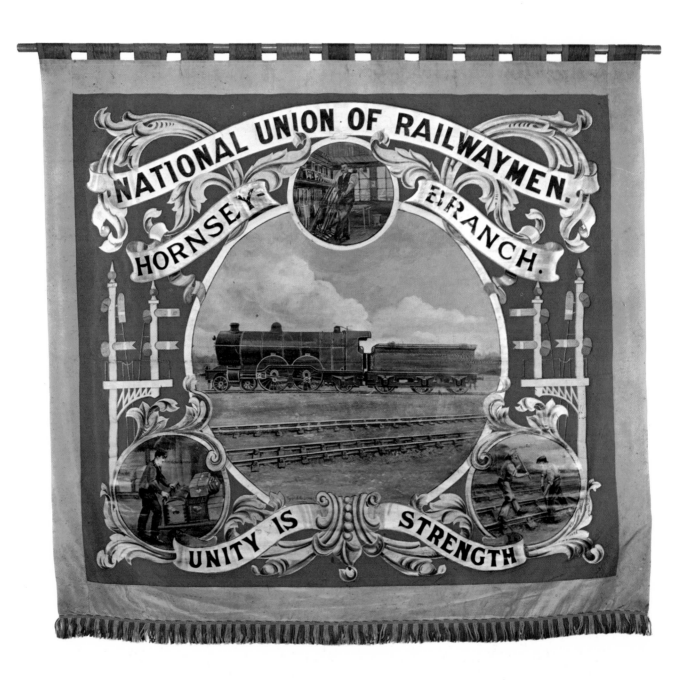

The Cardiff, Penarth and Barry Coal Trimmers' Association was formed in 1888 and it is believed that the banner dates from that period. The union was never very large, averaging some 1,500 members during most of its life before amalgamation with the Transport and General Workers' Union in 1968. The banner was painted by a Cardiff artist, W.E. Britton.

The Iron and Steel Trades Confederation is one of the few trade unions whose banners have actually been painted by an exhibitor of the Royal Academy. In 1919, as a result of enquiries from certain branches, the executive committee resolved to commission the design of an emblem and 'moderate-sized banners'. After lengthy negotiations, Herbert J. Finn was given the order. Finn travelled to iron and steel plants and produced a series of paintings of the men working at the various aspects of the industry. He painted seven banners in all, one for each division of the union. Each banner was double-sided and showed eleven different scenes. The BISAKTA general account for the quarter ended 31 March 1921 shows 'emblems and copyright of same £2,222 11s. 0d.'. Exactly what the union got for their money is not clear, but Finn's original paintings still hang in Swinton House, the union HQ, and the banners are truly a work of art. These magnificent colours are loaned to branches when they are required for demonstrations or functions and the strict regulations governing their hire has ensured that the banners are still in mint condition.

Haggerston branch of the National Union of General and Municipal Workers banner depicts actual rank-and-file union members posed before the gas plant and sawmill where they were employed. Standing before the Grand Union Canal, they were painted holding the various tools used in their day-to-day work. The strange device held by the trade unionist in the centre is a piece of sounding equipment. The boilermaker's spanner and sack hook are easily identified but the purpose of the other implements is not known. The banner was painted shortly after the First World War.

◀ One of Herbert J. Finn's watercolour studies for the banners of the Iron and Steel Trades Confederation.

The diverse activities of the members of the National Union of General Workers are well illustrated in the seven work scenes on the face of this sixty-five-year-old banner. They are reminders of the vast amount of manual labour that would now be handled by machines. The sawyers cutting an enormous tree trunk by hand, the brewers' dray without a forklift or tail-lift in sight, the road repairer with his pick and the women laundry workers with hand irons heated by gas. The centre painting shows workers leaving the Huntley and Palmer biscuit factory at Reading where many of the local union members worked.

The mining scene emblazoned on the seventy-year-old banner of the Hanley branch of the North Stafford Miners' Federation is illustrated in George Tutill's catalogue of 1895. Used on a number of banners for lodges in the Midlands and the North, it gives a strong impression of the work of the collier in that age. Note the miner at the foot of the picture, stripped to the waist, lying full length to work a narrow seam.

This must be the banner that has everything. The classic Victorian love of titles which leave nothing in doubt, three slogans, five work scenes and a delightful drawing of Unity, symbolised by two hand-clasping figures. It is interesting to observe the women workers handling the salt blocks in the bottom right illustration on the front of the banner. Women workers, textile trade unions apart, are hardly ever to be seen on banners made before 1900. The paintings leave no doubt about the arduous and obnoxious nature of the work, and capture perfectly the working conditions of the industry. The banner was deposited with the Salt Museum, Northwich, in 1980.

The effects of twelve hours of arduous toil are contrasted with the social benefits of a shorter working day on this Tutill banner made for the Lofthouse branch of the Yorkshire Miners' Association. A fine example of a Victorian picture story, the banner was probably made shortly before the First World War to replace an earlier colour on the same theme. There are accounts of early banners of the Durham Miners' Association bearing a similar illustration and the Wigan Miners' Association formed in 1862 carried a virtually identical picture. Tutill's catalogue of 1895 explains the design 'showing the difference in a miner's life after twelve hours or eight hours work. In one, he returns home too exhausted to care for his food and his child is in its nightdress ready for bed; while in the other, he is able to sit down comfortably to his tea and evening paper and to enjoy the rest he has so well earned.'

A new banner in traditional style, painted in 1953 for the London Cooperative branch of the Union of Shop, Distributive and Allied Workers. The banner was painted by Herbert Sharpe, a former employee of Tutill's, who established himself as a freelance banner artist, working mainly for Tutill's, after the Second World War. The registration number of the electric van seen on the banner is HS 1953, which was Sharpe's way of signing and dating many of the banners he produced. The banner depicts the London Cooperative Society headquarters at Stratford, London, and shows the differing jobs undertaken by USDAW members in the employment of the society.

Agricultural workers are among the most enthusiastic banner bearers to be found in British trade unionism, rivalling the miners and railwaymen with their large numbers of banners. Following the Second World War, almost every county ordered a new banner and many banners made between the wars still survive. Old and new banners alike depict the pride of the farm worker in a range of skills from hedging to driving a combine harvester. Only one banner of the National Union of Agricultural Labourers and Rural Workers formed in 1910 is known to survive, that of the Mulbarton and District which was found in a garden shed by Wilfred Page, a union official, in 1976. No banners at all of Joseph Arch's National Agricultural Labourers' Union formed in 1872 have been found, yet some must surely still exist. Perhaps somewhere in the attic of a Warwickshire cottage there is at least one relic of the 'great awakening of Hodge'.

TITLES MOTTOES AND BADGES

The Chelmsford branch banner of the
National Union of General Workers is
a coloured version of Walter Crane's
black and white illustration 'A Garland
for May Day' drawn for the *Clarion* in
1895.

'A Garland for May Day',
an illustration by Walter Crane.

'United brassworkers are invincible'
proclaims the banner of the National
Society of Metal Mechanics. The motto
is illustrated by the fable of the sticks.
More than sixty years old, the banner
was over-painted when the name of the
union changed from the National
Society of Brass and Metal Mechanics.

Designed by Mountain and Molehill
for the Society of Graphic and Allied
Trades and made by Turtle and Pearce
in 1968.

Members of the Film Production, TV and Laboratory Workers' branches of this union came together to make their banner in 1971. Carried on the great TUC demonstration against the Industrial Relations Bill, the banner has since been used in demonstrations throughout Britain.

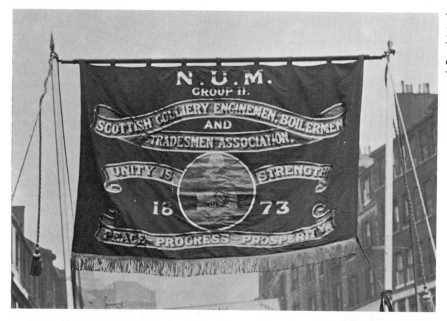

The banner of the Scottish Colliery Enginemen, Boilermen and Tradesmen was made by the drapery department of the Scottish Cooperative Wholesale Society in 1960.

The National League of the Blind was formed in 1899, its chief object being 'assistance to members in cases of strikes, distress and unemployment, legal assistance and funeral benefits'. This banner, which dates from the turn of the century is the only one of the League's many branch banners to have survived from that period.

Delegates of the National Union of
Clerks at the union conference in Hull,
1914. The union was formed in 1890
and the Hull branch banner would
seem to date from that decade.

The Manchester Divisional banner of the Union of Shop, Distributive and Allied Workers was made in 1955 to replace the old banner of the National Union of Distributive and Allied Workers, outdated by the amalgamation of three distributive workers' unions in 1945.

The old banner of the National Union of Insurance Workers was destroyed when the union offices were blitzed in 1942 and no photograph has been traced. This banner was made in 1971.

'Tune in to unity' reads the motto on the banner of the Musicians' Union, now lost, carried in the 1938 London May Day march. The union has no idea of the present whereabouts of the banner.

The banner of the Watford Typographical Society was made in 1949 by a local Watford firm which is unhappily no longer in business. Surely they deserved to succeed if this well-designed banner, with exceptionally fine typography for a hand-written job, was typical of their work. The design commemorates the founding of the Typographical Association in 1849.

The forerunner of the Post Office Engineering Union was the Postal Telegraph Linemen's Association founded in 1887. In existence during the peak period of banner making it is certain that the old union must have owned a number of traditional banners, though none appears to have survived. The London City branch banner uses a composite London skyline for visual identity and a badge bearing the clasped hands of unity as a symbol of intent. The union became known as the National Communication Union in 1985.

The Sussex District banner of the Amalgamated Society of Woodworkers now hangs permanently in Chichester Cathedral. The banner was dedicated by the Bishop of Chichester in 1968.

The banner of the Inland Revenue Staff Federation carried on an anti-racist demonstration in London in 1976. The origin of the union began with the Association of Tax Clerks founded in 1892. Affiliated to the TUC the banner of this 'black-coated' union is often to be seen on trade union demonstrations. The original banner of the union simply carried the initials IRSF in yellow and blue, the colours of the union.

The first and only banner of the Fire Brigades' Union. The banner was designed by a serving fireman and was made in 1947 (after considerable discussion about the estimated cost) by the firm of Toye (makers of royal standards) at a cost of £400. Embroidered in gold metal thread, the banner took a year to make and is without doubt the finest quality banner possessed by any trade union.

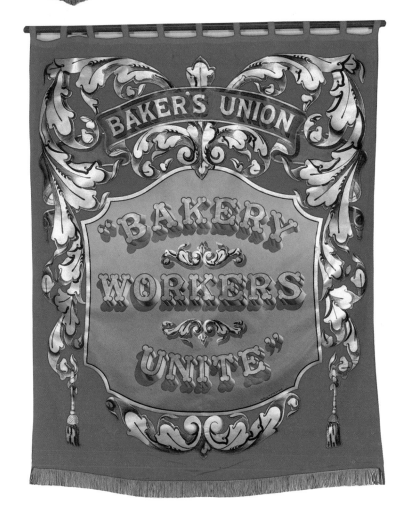

There is more than a touch of the fairground style in the superb lettering on the national banner of the Bakers' Union. In fact, the banner was only made after the Second World War, when Tutill's had moved to Chesham, but the ornate lettering, first used by the firm's founder more than a century ago, has hardly changed.

'Buy only the bread with the union label' proclaims the Yiddish slogan on the banner of the London Jewish Bakers' Union. Formed in 1905 to assist Russian and Polish immigrant bakers in London's East End, the union flourished in the days when there were as many as fifty Jewish bakers' shops between Aldgate Pump and Sidney Street. To ensure that only 'union bread' went into the homes of fellow trade unionists and sympathizers, every loaf from an organised shop had a paper label of postage-stamp size, similar in design to the centre part of the banner, pressed into the loaf. During early strikes for recognition there was bitter feeling towards those of the local Jewish community who dared to buy 'scab bread' as it was known, from non-union sweat shops. After the Second World War in a devastated and rapidly changing East London, young men rejected the night work and arduous conditions of the trade. With the increasing development of machine baking the union membership declined in numbers. For many years prior to its dissolution in 1970 it was Britain's smallest union, paying only 18*s.* per year affiliation fee, and was affectionately known as the 'Baker's Dozen'.

The obverse of the banner depicts two Jewish bakers clasping hands in solidarity and proclaims the union's affiliation to the Trades Union Congress, the International Federation of Trades Unions and the London Trades Council. Its mottoes call for the abolition of night work, the eight-hour day and proclaim that 'Labour is international'.

Each of the sixteen divisions of the Draughtsmen's and Allied Technicians' Association possessed a similar banner, based on the set-square design. The union became part of the Technical and Supervisory Section of the Amalgamated Union of Engineering Workers in 1970.

The old banner of the London District Committee of the Tobacco Workers' Union was made in the 1920s. It was last carried in public in 1939.

'Out of darkness into light', another scriptural motto, 1 Peter 2:9, on the banner of the Cannock Chase Mineworkers' Union. The light in this case was the union, leading to a better life. The banner was made sometime during the 1930s.

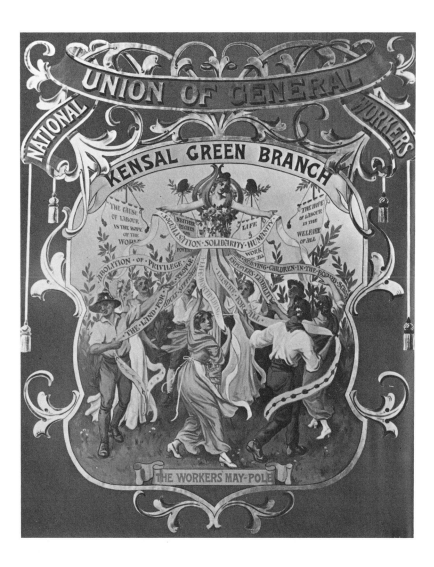

Mottoes and slogans have always featured prominently on the banners of the trade unions. At first, translation of the Latin mottoes of the guilds sufficed, but from this soon developed phrases and slogans which crystallized the aims of the unions and the hopes and demands of their members. These illustrations from banners of unions for 'general workers' were made between 1910 and 1920 but take their romantic symbolism from Walter Crane. The Women Workers' section of the Workers' Union and the Kensal Green branch of the National Union of General Workers derive their illustrations from 'The Workers' Maypole' drawn by Crane in 1894. 'International Solidarity of Labour' was also by Crane in 1889, and the Aldershot branch of the Workers' Union's 'angel of trade unionism' stems from Crane's famous painting, *Freedom*, exhibited in 1885. The mottoes of the nineteenth century were still considered valid in the 1920s. 'No starving children in the board schools' is a cry from the halcyon days of Tory Britain when free school dinners and milk were only a worker's dream. 'Shorten working day and lengthen life' is a plea from a labourers' union at a time when men were used as power for the digging, lifting, carrying, mixing, breaking and building that

today is done largely by machines. The hope expressed on all the banners is for brotherhood, friendship and peace. The cry is for the abolition of privilege and the demand for basic rights to give a quality of life commensurate with a civilised and cultured society, work for the common good and not for private profit, leisure for all and not for a privileged few. In their desperate lives of poverty and hardship, the slogans are for the 'triumph of labour, the hope of the world'.

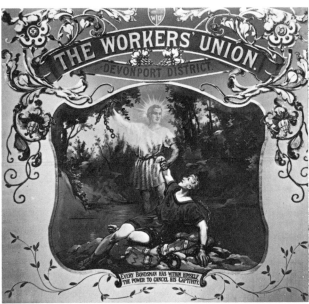

The Paddington branch banner of the Union of Post Office Workers may be of the home-made variety but it has a graphic quality and a certain naïve charm. It was made in 1947 at the instigation of Monty Banks, the branch secretary, and Harry Rowe, an active member of the UPW. While delivering letters in Queensway, Banks met a Czech refugee commercial artist, who offered to make the banner. Banks sketched out the design which shows the UPW emblem, the caduceus of Mercury, and added the familiar pillar box and telegraph poles which reflect the amalgamation of the Telegraph Clerks' Association and the United Kingdom Postal Clerks' Association into the UPW. The banner cost £16 and the money was raised by raffling a bottle of whisky. In true union tradition the banner was unfurled at a public house, The Laurie Arms.

The Association of Scientific Workers was formed on 17 February 1918 at a meeting of scientists held in the rooms of Dr Kidd in St John's College, Cambridge. The association is now part of the Association of Scientific, Technical and Managerial Staffs; the present whereabouts of the AScW banner is unknown. This photograph, however, shows the banner, which was frequently used, being carried in May 1967 outside the employer's offices in Davenport Road, Coventry, during a strike of union members of the Standard Triumph Company, for higher pay. The banner had yellow lettering on a blue ground.

This banner was made in 1963 by Harold Colley, a Manchester branch secretary, for a demonstration against the 'Beeching Cuts'. It is used as a drape at the union's annual conference and was carried at the TUC-organised march against the Industrial Relations Bill in 1971. None of the banners of the union's predecessor, the Railway Clerks' Association, formed in 1897, have yet been located.

One of the few trade union banners to have been carried at the 'Battle of Cable Street' in 1936, when the Left united to stop Mosley from marching his Fascists through the predominantly Jewish area of East London. The original banner of the union, formed in 1866, has been lost.

The London and Home Counties Divisional Council banner of the Chemical Workers' Union. It is believed to have been made in 1936 when the union shortened its title from the National Union of Drug and Chemical Workers. The union became part of the Transport and General Workers' Union in 1972.

To mark the amalgamation of the National Union of Foundry Workers, the Ironfounding Workers' Association and the United Metal Founders' Society into the Amalgamated Union of Foundry Workers in 1946, new banners were made for each of the thirteen districts the following year. The banner shown is that of the London district. The union amalgamated with the AEU in 1967 to form the Amalgamated Union of Engineering and Foundry Workers. Since October 1984 the foundry workers have been part of the Amalgamated Union of Engineering Workers (Engineering Foundry and Construction Section).

'Construction not destruction' reads the motto on the banner of the Amalgamated Union of Building Trade Workers, made just after the Second World War. Here, in 1951, the banner is carried on a demonstration against German rearmament.

The 'circular saw badge' of the National Union of Packing Case Makers is featured as the centre painting of the Kingsland branch (London) banner of the union, made by Tutill's shortly after the First World War. The obverse depicts two workers, one operating a bandsaw, the other nailing a packing case. The union amalgamated with the Amalgamated Society of Woodworkers in 1965.

This Civil Service Union banner is painted in red, white and blue. It was made in 1971 and carried on the TUC protest march against the Industrial Relations Bill.

The Burns quotation is well chosen for the Seafield branch banner of the National Union of Mineworkers, as the design on the face of the banner depicts people of all races united in peace and brotherhood.

RESURGENCE

The London Region banner of the Union of Construction, Allied Trades and Technicians was designed by John Midgley of Chippenham Designs in 1976. The banner cost £400 and is a fine example of modern design combined with traditional features, including the practice of craft unions of displaying the work skills of their members. The banner did bring initial criticism from some of the union's leadership as the men depicted at work on a construction site are not wearing safety helmets. The union was formed in 1971 from an amalgamation of three key unions in the building industry, the Amalgamated Union of Building Trade Workers, the Amalgamated Society of Woodworkers and the National Union of Building Trade Operatives.

The banner was photographed on a joint TUC and Labour Party demonstration against racism in London, 1976.

With the Tolpuddle Martyrs' gate as its centre painting, the Southern Division branch banner of the Union of Shop, Distributive and Allied Workers' banner was appropriately first paraded at the annual Tolpuddle rally in 1973. Made by Turtle and Pearce at a cost of approximately £750, the design was a cooperative effort, following an appeal to members for ideas and the establishment of a banner subcommittee of the Divisional Council. The Tolpuddle Martyrs monument lies within the area covered by the Southern Division of the union and is timeless in its relevance to trade unionism. Brighton Pavilion, Dover Castle and the county insignia of the eight divisions of the union complete the imagery. Carried at many demonstrations since its inaugural parade and beginning to show signs of wear, the banner was renovated by Turtle and Pearce in 1984. The Southern Division's banner was the first new USDAW banner for some years and its appearance brought a quick response from the union's remaining seven Divisional Areas, all of whom commissioned new banners.

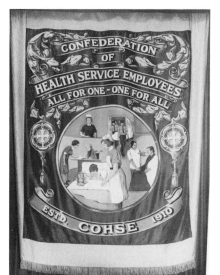

Formed in 1910 as the National Asylum Workers' Union by seventeen nurses meeting in the Mason's Arms, Whitfield, Lancashire, the Confederation of Health Service Employees adopted its present title following an amalgamation in 1946 between the Mental Hospital and Institutional Workers' Union and the Hospitals and Welfare Services Union. The COHSE national banner, depicting male and female staff engaged in various hospital tasks, was designed and made in 1978 by Toye, Kenning and Spencer. The cost of the design was £500 and the cost of manufacture, £1,348. With the accessories, poles, ropes, cords, cover and box, the total bill was £2,065.

The Wessex District Council banner of the National Union of Railwaymen was designed and made by Southampton art teacher, Catriona Christison, in 1977 and first paraded at the annual Tolpuddle Martyrs' rally that year. The banner is embroidered in satinised fabrics on a green background and depicts the Wessex wyvern rampant holding the NUR badge with the motto 'Workers of the world unite'. Parts of the dragon have been quilted to give form to the illustration. Ms Christison, now retired, spent her working life teaching art in the Southampton area and was a tutor at the Southampton College of Art when she made the banner. The cost of £300 to cover the materials used was raised by donations from NUR branches and a balance paid from the district council funds of the union.

Although NATSOPA amalgamated with the Society of Graphical and Allied Trades in 1982, to form SOGAT '82, the *Sun* Machine chapel retained its NATSOPA banner from a sense of pride and loyalty to the old union. Made to mark the tenth anniversary of the *Sun* Machine chapel when Rupert Murdoch launched his new tabloid in 1969, the banner was unveiled to the membership in the ballroom of the Hilton Hotel at a dinner to celebrate the first ten years of the paper. Made by Turtle and Pearce in 1979 at a cost of £600 the design was the idea of two union officials, Johnny McDonald and Brian Henderson. Until the dispute with News International in 1985, the banner was kept in the *Sun* building in the heart of Fleet Street and used mainly at functions to mark the retirement of long serving members.

A banner that illustrates an historical event. First paraded in 1977, the Department for National Savings branch banner of the Civil and Public Services Association commemorates the first national strike by the CPSA on 23 February 1973. Called as a protest against the pay freeze policy of the Conservative government led by Edward Heath, more than a quarter of a million civil servants supported the twenty-four hour stoppage.

The illustration on the banner shows strikers marching past the Glasgow office where over 3,500 CPSA members are employed. The banner they are depicted carrying is the original banner of the DNS branch, simply lettered in black on white canvas. The new banner was painted by George Filer, a union member, and stitched together by his sister. The total cost of materials was £241, the major portion being for the poles and fittings, which came to £160.

The history of the National Graphical Association is traced on their banner by recording the main amalgamations of societies that joined together to form the present union. The NGA stemmed directly from the Provincial Typographical Association founded in 1849, although associations of journeymen printers are known to have existed from 1785. The banner design was the idea of John Johnson, a union member of Head Office staff of the NGA, and was produced by Chippenham Designs in 1979 at a total cost of £1,100. An unusual feature of the banner is that it carries the same design on both sides. With some foresight, the banner was made with the last scroll blank to allow for the anticipated amalgamation with the Society of Lithographic Artists, Designers, Engravers and Process Workers which was concluded in 1982 when the union became known as the National Graphical Association (1982).

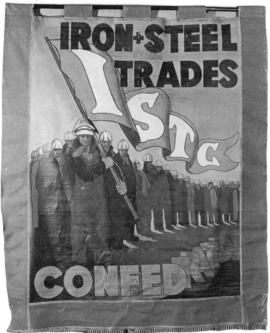

Andrew Turner, the painter of the Manchester branch banner of the General and Municipal Workers' Union, was a post-graduate student of the Royal Academy. Commissioned in 1978, the banner was completed in 1979, the artist working in close and sometimes controversial liaison with representatives of the two-thousand-strong, militant 115 branch. Turner's brief was 'What we have in mind is a banner that shows the strength of us all . . . I mean the working class.' Turner submitted his written proposals together with large scale working drawings to a delegation who accepted the principle of the design but argued over the use of a quotation by Marx, 'Workers of the world unite – you have nothing to lose but your chains', as being too communist, and his choice of blue as a background colour as too conservative. Eventually, Turner had his artistic way with the colour, but changed the quotation from Marx to one by Engels, 'It is not the lowness of wages which forms the fundamental evil, but the wages system itself', giving as his reason the close association of Engels with Manchester.

The banner, which cost approximately £550, was unveiled before two hundred shop stewards, the majority of whom liked the design, though a good number remained unhappy about the 'conservative blue' background. One young steward, struggling to express his feelings about the banner, exclaimed, 'He's like the Incredible Hulk, smashing everything that stands in the way of the working class.' The name stuck, and the banner is affectionately referred to as the 'Incredible Hulk' banner by hundreds of Manchester trade unionists.

The banner was the first of Turner's illustrated banners for trade unions and has been followed by a number of highly acclaimed works. Discriminating in the commissions he accepts and steadfastly refusing to work in the nineteenth century romantic style still favoured by some unions, his productions in recent years include banners for the Chesterfield Glassworks Joint Shop Stewards Committee, NALGO and Turner's own favourite, the Joint Trades Unions banner for the Stocksbridge Steelworkers.

This powerful banner for the Iron and Steel Trades Confederation was painted by Bryan Blumer of Corby Community Arts. It was made during the national steel strike of 1980 when the union realised that their old banner, unused for many years, was too fragile and faded to serve for demonstrations. The replacement was rushed through in record time and only intended to serve as a temporary banner until a permanent replacement was commissioned after the strike. The banner was made for a nominal sum to cover the cost of the materials used.

Designed by Ken Sprague and made by his sister, Pat Meaden, the National and Local Government Officers' Association banner was commissioned in 1977 and completed in 1980. The design draws upon four symbols from the union's old badge, the scales of justice and the lamp of learning, the quill pen, replaced by a 1920s pen to remind us of the power of the woman's vote, the cornucopia, replaced by a fruit tree representing life and growth through all seasons of the year, and the sun and moon standing for round-the-clock work by NALGO members in the public services. These services are depicted in the middle ground of the banner which illustrates the tearing down of the old and the building of better community life and services. The flower emblems of England, Scotland and Wales represent the national organisation of the union and the services it covers. The ballot box represents not only democracy in the union but its members wider services in running the nation's democratic elections.

The banner has two personal touches: a small but friendly worm at work among the fruit tree of life, for as Pat Meaden says, 'Nothing is perfect', and a sealed package containing the legend of the banner and the documentation of the unveiling ceremony sewn into the banner itself.

Measuring 3.66 x 2.44 m, the banner is made up of twenty-eight vibrant fabrics chosen by Pat Meaden from John Lewis's Oxford Street store. Perhaps the commitment of the seamstress in making the banner is best summed up in Pat's own words: 'There were times when I felt very isolated sitting at the machine, but for that I am grateful, as it made me think. As I made the female hand holding the pen I noticed that it came just above the ballot box and my mind turned to the many who fought so hard that we might have the right to use it. That day I put the cross that registers the vote a little sideways so that it also reads as a plus sign. Just as a gesture, for them.'

After nearly three years of hard work the £2,000 banner was unveiled on 23 May 1980 at a ceremony at Nalgo House, London. The photograph shows the banner being paraded in London 27 October 1985 during the TUC demonstration in defence of the Welfare State. Such is the size and weight of the banner that it requires a wheeled carriage for support. Two smaller versions of the same design have been made in recent years that are suitable for carrying.

Made in 1980, the banner of the National Union of Hosiery and Knitwear Workers is based upon the design of the old union emblem, made in the 1880s by the lithographers, Alexander Gow. The centre illustration depicts a knitting room with a male operative to the machine and women at a hand bench. The design incorporates the five major societies from which the present union stems: 1776, Stocking Makers' Association, 1812, Union Society of Framework Knitters, 1890, Women's Hosiery Workers' Union, 1921, Hinckley, Leicester, Ilkeston, Loughborough, Nottingham District Unions and finally, 1945, the National Union of Hosiery Workers. Even these are only representative of the many hosiery unions that rose and fell in the East Midlands during the nineteenth century before consolidation in comparatively recent times.

The single-sided banner, unusual with its semi-circular lower edge, was made by Toye, Kenning and Spencer of Bedworth at a cost of £834 plus a further £220 for the wooden case, crosspoles, uprights and guide ropes. The banner was photographed in London, 11 August 1984, at a demonstration in support of the miners' strike.

The Red Flag is unfurled over the House of Lords on the Association of Clerical, Technical and Supervisory Staffs banner of the Transport and General Workers' Union. The banner was made in 1985 for the 1/427 branch, the first union branch formed in Parliament to organise employees of Members of Parliament and Members of the European Parliament. It was designed and made by Thalia and Ian Campbell with help from Linda Norris. The Campbells are a family group of mother, father and daughter trading as Campbell Design and have made more than seventy banners for progressive causes since 1972. The union branch sent a rough pencil sketch of what they wanted illustrated on their banner, but it was the Campbells who suggested setting the hands of Big Ben at five minutes to midnight, a CND reference to nuclear disaster, the Red Flag over the Lords as a comment on their eventual abolition and the addition of the female symbol on the obverse of the banner to make women feel welcome in the union. The Campbells' banners are all sewn, not painted, appliqué being their chosen technique for banner production, and neighbours who enjoy sewing are enlisted to help on the more ambitious projects.

The banner was charged at £150, a purely nominal sum, as a Parliamentary banner was seen as a means of publicity. A true costing would have been nearer £500.

A banner for our time, the first British trade union banner to feature a silicon chip. If the old tradition of parading banners contrasts strongly with the new technology, the pride of workers for their craft skills and for the products of their labours remains unchanged. The banner of the Power and Engineering Birmingham District Committee of the Transport and General Workers' Union was made in 1982 by Turtle and Pearce, the successors to Tutill's. The design was conceived by John Turner, a member of 5/709 branch of the union and then taken to a finished stage by Deborah Burton, a graphic designer. The banner was ordered on 30 October 1981 and delivered to Transport House, Birmingham, on the 29 June 1982. The total cost of £2,240.75 was raised by regular contributions from local branches and individuals, a generous sum from the regional committee and the inevitable monthly raffles.

Among the major demonstrations on which the banner has been carried the union proudly lists the Health Service dispute, 1982, the Midlands campaign for jobs, 1982, the TUC Day of Action in support of the Health Workers, London, 1982, the Birmingham Day of Action for the Health Workers in November the same year and the People's March for Jobs, London, 1983.

The obverse of the banner carries the mottoes 'If I lose mine honour, I lose myself', 'Strength of mind is exercise, not rest', and an old union motto 'Be united by heart, hand and deed'.

Detail from the Region No. 5 banner of the Transport and General Workers' Union. The banner bears the verse:

Our masters all, a godly crew,
Whose hearts throb for the poor,
Their sympathies assure us, too,
If our demands were fewer,
Most generous souls! But please
  observe,
What they enjoy from birth
Is all we ever had the nerve
To ask, that is THE EARTH.

The tradition of paying homage to working class leaders on trade union banners is maintained on the 1984 banner of the Lanarkshire Association of the Educational Institute of Scotland. The two pioneers selected for tribute are Robert Owen, 1771-1859, and John MacLean, 1879-1923. Owen, famed as the inspirer of the modern cooperative movement and for his model mills at New Lanark, was also an educational reformer and the innovator of nursery schools. John MacLean, the errand boy who became a school teacher, was a revolutionary socialist and outstanding marxist educator. Repeatedly imprisoned for remaining steadfast to his socialist principles, MacLean was honoured by the new Soviet government by being appointed Russian Consul to Scotland in January 1918.

The banner, seen being carried in London in November 1985 during the teachers' pay dispute, was designed by Norman Bissell, MA (Hons), who was president of the Lanarkshire Association in 1984. Produced by a team of artists at Chippenham Designs, the total cost of the banner was £1,950.

Painted in acrylic colours on 9 oz. cotton duck canvas, the West London District Committee banner of the engineering section of the AUEW is the work of artist Sonya Walters. Born in Birmingham, she graduated from Chelsea School of Art in 1964 and has taught art in London schools for the past twenty years. Using her skill as a painter, Sonya Walters made her first banner to commemorate the Cuban building workers who were killed during the American invasion of Grenada. The banner now hangs in Cuba. She has only recently started to paint trade union banners, and the AUEW banner was made in early 1985 at a cost of £600.

The contemporary design draws on the union tradition of depicting work and products of the skills of the union members. Encompassed within a cog, there are four smaller cogs in the design which shows various workers, a black toolmaker, a woman engineer and mechanic and a cameo of tribute to the victory of the strikers in the Trico dispute, mainly Asian women. In common with the Region No.5 banner of the Transport and General Workers' Union, the AUEW banner illustrates Concorde, Heathrow Airport being an important place of employment for many of the West London members. The obverse of the banner is unusual, depicting four badges which trace the history of the union from the Amalgamated Society of Engineers in 1851 to the forming of the Amalgamated Union of Engineering Workers in 1971. The motto remains the old call of the AEU, 'Educate, organise, control'.

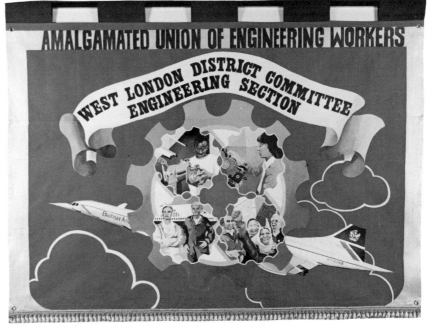

Of the 2,500 miners in Leicestershire, just thirty, mostly from Bagworth pit, came out on strike during the 1984-5 battle against pit closures. Referred to as 'the dirty thirty' by a working miner during a radio interview, the strikers proudly seized upon the title, using it first upon a badge and subsequently on their banner. In fact, there were two banners made for the Leicestershire strikers during the dispute, the first, a simple design bearing the words 'Leicestershire miners for the strike' and carrying the image of a Davy lamp, was made by the Leicestershire support group at the unemployed centre in Charles Street. 'The Dirty Thirty' banner was designed and made by Chippenham Designs and incorporates the two badges made in support of the strike. The banner was delivered in June 1984 and carried at the Durham Miners' Gala that year and at many demonstrations throughout the strike. The cost of the banner was subsidised by Chippenham Designs, the staff themselves contributing towards the final reduced price of £450. The obverse of the banner is plain, but it is hoped to inscribe the names of the thirty miners who supported the National Union of Mineworkers during the long and bitter fight. They are

Malcolm Pinnegar (Benny)
Mick (Richo) Richmond
Darren Moore
Dave Douglas
Phil Smith
Cliff (Geek) Jeffery
Nigel Jeffery
Bobby Girvan
Sammy Girvan
Mick Poli
Alan (Chunk) Findell
Ron McKillop
Brian Pallett
Mark Findell
Melvin Elcock
Mick Barnes
John Chiswell
Andy (Bunny) Warren
Johnny Gamble
(Geordie) Bobby Howard
Billy Scott
Martin Concannon
Keith Mellin
Bob MacSporran
Barry Draycott
Charlie (Waggy) Burton
John Shirkie
Arthur Davies-Bater
Gordon Birkin
Gordon Smith

The banner, at present kept by striker, Dave Douglas, is eventually to be deposited with a museum.

Made during the great miners' strike of 1984-5, the banner of the Goldthorpe branch of the Yorkshire area of the NUM shows miners driving off rats whose faces are likenesses of Prime Minister Margaret Thatcher, Chairman of the National Coal Board, Ian Macgregor and Energy Secretary, Peter Walker. They are flanked by two other rats, a bewigged judge and a policeman. The face of the banner carries portraits of strike committee members of the branch, Barry Miller, 'Daz' Farr, Joe Gaskill, Phil James and Frank Calvert, their clenched fists raised above a placard bearing the words 'no surrender'. Painted by Dave Bank, the banner was started in November 1984 and completed in January 1985, Bank charging only £98 to cover the cost of materials used. The photograph, taken on a CND demonstration in July 1985, shows branch president, Barry Miller, delegate, Phil James, Monsigneur Bruce Kent (then general secretary of CND) and committeeman, Pat Miskell. The banner is still in use as the official banner of the Goldthorpe branch.

INDEX